Grour
Christ

M. Desborough. (13)

Groundwork of Christian Spirituality

Gordon S. Wakefield

EPWORTH PRESS

To Mike Brearley
cricketer, analyst and dear friend

0 7162 0545 9

First published 2001
by Epworth Press
20 Ivatt Way
Peterborough, PE3 7PG

Typeset by Rowland Phototypesetting Ltd,
Bury St Edmunds, Suffolk
Printed and bound in Great Britain by Biddles Ltd,
Guildford and King's Lynn

Contents

Preface

This book has been some time in the making. This has been an advantage because it has enabled me to consult important works of spirituality published in the 1990s. I include, especially with regard to the medieval period, Eamon Duffy's *The Stripping of the Altars*, Bernard McGinn's volumes on *The Presence of God* and Denys Turner's *The Darkness of God*. There is also William Johnston's *Mystical Theology: The Science of Love*. For the period between the conversions of John Wesley and William Wilberforce there is D. Bruce Hindmarsh's *John Newton and the English Evangelical Tradition*. In the last two chapters I have drawn on my 1969 book, *The Life of the Spirit and the World of Today*, and hither and thither I have used *A Dictionary of Christian Spirituality* which I edited for SCM Press in 1983. I have also profited much from conversations over seven years with Gordon Mursell, now Provost of Birmingham Cathedral, on his forthcoming, mammoth *History of English Spirituality*. He also commented encouragingly on the prospectus of this book. Graham Slater read the earlier chapters in 1994 and I have incorporated his helpful comments. I mention all these with gratitude, as I do the co-operation of the Rev. Gerald Burt and the unfailing help of my wife. They are not, of course, responsible for my errors and limitations.

Gordon S. Wakefield

What is Spirituality?

'Spirituality' is a word much used in our time. It is an umbrella term under which many diverse features of religious experience may jostle one another: prayer in all its forms, worship, praxis, discipline and the stages of the religious life. It carries suggestions of a world beyond the mundane and the material, of ways of holiness, of growth in grace by means which deliver us from the frustrations of the intellectual quest and from debating those issues of academic theology in which, like Milton's fallen angels, we 'find no end in wandering mazes lost'. Some feel, though, that spirituality may be an escape into a kind of nirvana from engagement with the world and human life, the problems of faith in God, politics, economics and the daily round. It may even be 'a flight of the alone to the alone' and emphasize the first great commandment of Jesus – to love God, at the expense of the second – to love our neighbour.

My own rather crude definition would be to say that our spirituality is 'what makes us tick'. It is the sum of forces, influences, beliefs, disciplines, conscious or unconscious, which possess us, determine our motives and behaviour and shape our personalities.

This is very relevant to our life in this world, though it presupposes that there is in men and women a capacity for what is beyond the concerns of time, for an Ultimate Reality. In the words of Elihu in Job 32.8, there is 'a spirit in a human being'. In Hebrew belief, this is inbreathed by the Almighty. According to the young speaker, it gives understanding, intelligence. It controls our thoughts and actions. It is closely akin to what we call mind. Unlike Scripture, we make a distinction between mind and spirit and confine the former to the activities of systematic thought and conscious reason. We would think of the mind as the source of intellectual processes, like weighing evidence or solving problems, whether the latter be crossword puzzles, mathematical equations, or the dilemmas of ethics. The Bible would regard these as spiritual activities, though spirit is a more comprehensive term which includes what modern psychology calls the unconscious and what is beyond reason, the irrational, the instinctive and the mystical. The spirit is open to what is outside the psyche. The metaphor of possession is significant as is the analogy with intoxication. There may be an enthusiasm, an exuberance, a rapture, and actions which go beyond rational calculation and which transcend the self. There may be deep inward peace, but also disturbance, a troubling of the waters of the mind. For the Christian there is also another dimension. Spirituality marks an identifiable series of stages in the progress of the individual towards union with God. It is marked by growth towards Christlikeness and has consequences in deeds and words.

Spirituality, however, is not necessarily Christian or even good. The inbreathing and the possession are not always of the God of the Bible and the Christian faith. There are evil spirits as well as good. 'Spirituality is not always synonymous with Christian and the training of the soul in Christian faith requires as much weaning and purging from 'spiritual' movements in general as from vital urges and entanglements with things.'[1] The Buddha and Muhammad were as much spiritual beings as Christ; Hitler and Stalin as Dietrich Bonhoeffer and Mother Teresa. Saddam Hussain is as much a spiritual being as Desmond Tutu. National Socialism, Marxist Communism, Islamic Fundamentalism are spiritual movements. In *An Evil Cradling*, the account of his activity as a hostage, Brian Keenan describes how his guards would enter into states of ecstasy through chants and monotonous repetition of the words of the

Koran, a 'holy insanity' which not only drove Keenan and his fellow hostages to distraction but could be succeeded by outbursts of violence. Keenan came to see that this in fact expressed a deep melancholy and a desperate need. There are parallels in Christian history. Christian spirituality is of 'power, love and self-discipline' (or as the Authorized Version has it, 'sound mind').[2] But this has not always been evident among Christians. The Russian writer Maxim Gorky (1868–1936) has told how his grandfather, God-fearing, church-going, Bible-reading, devoted to the martyrs and saints, would beat his gentle, kindly wife until her hairpins were driven into her skull. Russian liturgy and icons were compatible with great brutality, smiting one's own breast in penitence and kicking one's wife in fury.[3]

Today there is much traffic with 'spirits'. Witchcraft has vogue, mediums do good business, ouija boards are prevalent not least among the young. Paganism is rehabilitated even among some Christians. Many would feel with Wordsworth 'I'd rather be a pagan/Suckled in a creed outworn' than to be blind to the wonders of nature or be party to its exploitation in the interests of predatory humankind. This is important and will occupy us later. It is a reaction to the triumph of technology and the belief that everything can be explained. The Charismatic Movement, which is by no means an exclusively Christian phenomenon, is in part, a counter to the 'lust for intelligibility' which has among other things prompted the modern revisions of forms of worship. To approach God in language 'understanded of the people' was an aim of sixteenth-century Reformation, as the archaic phrase implies. It is laudable, yet may reduce the mystery of the divine and be so down to earth as to imprison worshippers in a cage of modernity and this-worldliness which confines the soul and prevents it from soaring.

Paul had to contend at Corinth with a charismatic movement which in its extreme manifestation dispensed with Jesus and declared him anathema, accursed. This was not of the Holy Spirit. John, later followed in the Spiritual Exercises of Ignatius

Loyola, sixteenth-century founder of the Jesuits, gave an essential warning, 'My dear friends, do not trust every spirit, but
test the spirits to see whether they are from God'.[4]

Christian spirituality concerns the Christian life, its character
and the ways of its attainment, as inspired by the Holy Spirit
bestowed by the crucified, risen and ascended Christ. The
Spirit is the endless creativity of the incarnation which is all
one with the cross and resurrection. John says that the Spirit
was not given until Jesus was glorified, which happened by
means of his death. For Luke there is no Pentecost before
Calvary. Jesus, or what modern theologians call 'the Christ-
event', is central to Christian spirituality of all time, though
he has been seen from many perspectives and fulfilled himself
in many ways.

There has been development from the first days as the church
ventured beyond Bible lands. 'Culture', the pattern of beliefs,
customs, traditions which constitute a society, and geography
must not be ignored. The famous engraving by Dürer, the
Praying Hands, could have come only from Northern Europe,
not the Mediterranean lands. There it was customary to stand
for prayer with hands uplifted. The Praying Hands show the
posture of the feudal vassal before his lord. Climate and terrain
have influenced spirituality. The hot climates of the Far East
have been conducive to contemplation and a willingness to
accept the world the way it is, and not seek dynamic conversion
or change. And why did the fourteenth-century English mystics
flourish in the flat country of the East Midlands and East
Anglia? Mysticism has depended very much on geography,
on the Libyan desert, or the contours of Spain, or the bleak
north-eastern corner of Scotland. Rivers have been universally
significant, particularly in dry lands, from the great streams of
Mesopotamia which it was believed by the author of the second
creation story of Genesis flowed from the Paradise of God, to
the river of the water of life in Revelation, to say nothing of
the Ganges in Hinduism.

History has shaped spirituality: wars, power struggles, discoveries and the seeming accidents of human life. The effect

of the social sciences on the study of history, has led, in some quarters, to a determinism, a fatalism in which all is conditioned and the individual counts for nothing. Writing impartially on Fernand Braudel's *The Mediterranean and the Mediterranean World in the Age of Philip II*, Lawrence Stone has summarized the argument as follows:

> Compared with the vast inexorable tides of malaria, timber-cutting, soil erosion, demographic growth and decline, bullion transfers, or price revolution, the actions of emperors like Philip II are made to seem of only marginal importance in the evolution of the societies that developed around the great inland sea.[5]

This 'pragmatic pessimism' is not satisfactory. It cannot account for the dazzling achievements of the Italian Renaissance, which depended so much on individual genius and inspiration. Yet the discoveries and hypotheses of the social sciences cannot be discounted. Much does depend on the geographical and cultural milieu of a person's life, the state of society and the position of a man or woman within it, on expectations, sanitation, heredity, parental control, glands and hormones and physique. I myself felt a call to the ministry of the Methodist Church from my earliest years. I was convinced that it came directly from God, that he had sent me into the world to be a minister, though I did not allow myself to be distracted by illusions of greatness. In the years since, I have come to see myself as a 'period piece' of the type of those holy, precocious, rather delicate children of nineteenth-century religion deemed destined for God. Twentieth-century enlightenment saved me from the extremes of this. My home was no hothouse and I was encouraged to pursue academic studies and given a love of cricket. But no one is more a child of his time, though it gave me Christian faith, the matchless heritage of the Wesley hymns and a longing to be a preacher.

Individuals do arise, of whom I am not one, who may transcend the limitations of their epoch and psychology. They

form traditions or shatter or subtly change them. The spark of
their peculiar genius inflames others, perhaps a whole 'movement'. They make new discoveries about God and the meaning
of life or they become instruments of the revival of religion.
They may emphasize or exaggerate neglected aspects of faith,
like the followers of Montanus in the later second century,
who believed that their own prophetic enthusiasm was the
harbinger of the outpouring of the Holy Spirit, the Paraclete,
on the whole church, which was by now institutionalized,
morally accommodating and less fervent than in its beginnings.
The succession of such movements has been described in
Ronald Knox's brilliant book, *Enthusiasm*, and from a more
Protestant evangelical standpoint in R. Newton Flew's *The
Idea of Perfection in Christian Theology*.[6]

There has been throughout Christian history a dialectic and
a need of perpetual reformation accompanied by, in Lawrence
Stone's phrase, Christianity's 'perennial tendency to fission'.
Submerged and oppressed radical movements have from the
first made greater contributions than established hierarchies
have recognized. And this from the earliest Syrian ascetics
with their tendencies to the dualism associated with the Mani-
chees, the belief that they were involved in the cosmic struggle
between light and darkness and their harsh discipline, to the
Quakers and mid-seventeenth-century sects, the latter born to
bloom and droop, yet with influences on William Blake and
others.

Whatever some may feel, Christian spirituality is not a way
of escape from history or life in the world. We live as Christians at a particular time and place, and are formed by myriad
influences both inside and outside of ourselves. The life of the
Spirit means a constant pilgrimage with its heights and depths,
its wearisome plains and barren wilderness, the absence as
well as the presence of God, its darkness as well as light,
sensitivity both to beauty and joy and to perils and dangers,
an acceptance of the world and a renunciation of it.

Christ does not remove us from the world.[7] There is awareness among many in our time that Christian spirituality cannot

be divorced from creation itself, from politics, or from encounter with other faiths. It has always learned much from the world, though with danger of conformity. It must do so still. It can never forget that God's love for the world is the source of the incarnation and that Jesus Christ, his Son was in the world as God's Word had always been, and, though rejected, died for it to show the way of life and bring it home to God. The Word is present wherever there is good which triumphs over evil, or self is transcended in the love of God and neighbour. Yet there is that in Christianity which is distinctive and makes an offer hardly matched elsewhere and an absolute demand. Sometimes Christianity in its failures and distortions of the mind of Christ and its pristine gospel is rebuked by other faiths. It may in this be seen as one of many ways to God, but there is no other way like it with its story of the divine initiative, and a crucified carpenter, and of the Holy Spirit, the Lord the Giver of Life, received through his death to make his followers one with God and with each other.

Chapter 1

The New Testament

The New Testament is no unified manual of spirituality, but a wealth of scattered writings with varieties of Christian experience and theology. It cannot be understood without the references it frequently makes to the Hebrew scriptures and the history of Israel. Its God is the same, living, active, bound up with the history of his people, though creator of the ends of the earth, who is the origin and end of the whole cosmos. We shall see that Christians have had their own way of reading what for them has been the Old Testament, the record of the original covenants which God made with the Jews and which has always, in parts embarrassed some, from the heretic Marcion in the second century, Origen of Alexandria in the early-third century, to a modern scholar such as Robert Carroll, who thinks it so full of scandalous stories and so removed from our culture as to be unfit for Christian reading.[1] But the New Testament is of the same ethos and genre and a continuation of the same history, its expectations and hopes fulfilled in Jesus Christ.

It is important, though not easy, to try and distinguish between the spirituality of Jesus himself and that which results from the encounter with him through the proclamation of eye-witnesses or those who had been converted by their testimony. Paul may have been unique as the subject of a direct revelation, doubtless the consequences both of a violent hatred and a mystic's brooding on one who at first threatened his whole way of life and then came to win his wholehearted allegiance. The writers of the New Testament had all been brought into what Rowan Williams has called '"dramatic" relation with the subject of the (Christian) story', that is Jesus. The hearer is offered a new self-understanding or definition determined by his or her attitude towards Jesus and 'a place within the story itself, as recipient of forgiveness and of judgment, as colluding with the betrayal of Jesus and sharing in the power of the risen Lord'.[2] The difficulty lies in trying to decide what are the original sayings of Jesus and what are the interpretations of his life and teaching drawn out of the experience of those who had found their place in his continuing story.

The spirituality of Jesus

It is certain that Jesus himself stood in the tradition of the Jewish scriptures and the Hebrew ethical prophets. Of his own five prayers recorded in the Synoptic Gospels, two of the three from the cross are from the Psalms, one of despairing complaint (Mark 15.34; Matt. 27.46), the other of surrender into God's hands, whom he calls Father, as the Psalmist does not (Luke 23.46). Here we are on delicate ground historically, but though it is not possible to be sure that these are authentic prayers of Jesus from the cross – and they occur in different gospels written from different perspectives – we may affirm with complete confidence that Jesus prayed as his forbears had done. He was steeped in the Jewish scriptures and the Jewish Temple was dominant in his spirituality. Luke says he loved it from a boy and that no charge that he had foretold its destruction was brought against him at his trial. He ousted the traders to take possession of it for his own teaching in his last days. In all the other gospels there is more sense of his opposition to it as a symbol of institutionalism, exclusiveness, more concerned with rites which bolstered its power than with justice and the love of God. The true sacrifice is offered outside its gates, 'without a city wall'. The new temple is his body offered in death, 'a house of prayer for all nations'. In John 14.23, following on from the many mansions, individual rooms or apartments, of the Father's house in 14.2, 'the sanctuary or home of God which is in heaven, and was but incompletely revealed in the temple at Jerusalem, will descend upon each Christian believer'.[3] Here again it is not possible to distinguish between Jesus' own sayings and actions and the reflections of his followers upon him and his life and death.

Jesus' teaching about prayer may not have been as primary or as extensive as that of conventional holy men. According to St Luke's Gospel, Jesus had to be asked to give instruction in prayer, 'Lord teach us to pray, as John taught his disciples'.[4] He seems only to have given his disciples one form of prayer of his own. For the rest, the Hebrew Bible and especially the Psalms offered sufficient resources. When his direct teaching came, it was of petition rather than contemplation: 'Ask and you will receive; seek and you will find; knock and the door will be opened to you.'[5]

Jesus did not teach techniques of meditation. God is not to be encountered, as in Buddhism, through 'a sustained introspective awareness that leads to a perception of "the Self in the self"', but by prayer in the basic sense of conversation, asking'.[6] Again and again this is stressed in all four gospels, to the embarrassment of modern teachers of prayer who would relegate petition to the lower levels from which one must graduate to achieving pure contemplation through meditation. In fact petition is the prayer of faith which reaches its height in the commitment to one who can be addressed, though beyond words, who hears and answers prayer. He wants us to ask. His desire is to keep his people praying because their desire, the longing of their hearts, is for a personal relationship with him.

This view of prayer also recognizes God's ultimate sovereignty. The things of this life are not to be snatched for ourselves irrespective of the one from whom they come, to whom they rightly belong, or of the needs of others who have equal claims. What is more, petition is 'the test of our sincerity, a genuine dialogue with God in which we wrestle with him about concrete issues'.[7]

Persistence is all important. The answer may be 'No!' Did anyone have more prayers refused than Jesus Christ himself? According to St Mark's Gospel, he seems to have died with a cry of forsakenness on his lips. But he kept on praying in the words of the Psalmist even then. He asked 'why have you forsaken me?' but still spoke to 'my God'.

The saying 'Ask and you will receive', quoted from Luke 11.9 is preceded by the Parable of the Churlish Neighbour, who has to be denied sleep by his bread-seeking neighbour's incessant banging on his door before he meets his need. If for purely selfish reasons a human being will accede to his request, how much more will God give what we ask? Luke, however, possibly in awareness that material wants might not always be supplied, revises Matthew's version of what constitutes the gift, from 'good things' to 'the Holy Spirit'.[8] Yet one meaning of the prayer, 'Give us this day our daily bread' is 'Give us today bread enough for tomorrow', and it may be that the followers of Jesus will always receive the iron rations, the bare necessities of life, though they are not to make exorbitant demands, or ask for affluence and luxuries.

God is our Father in heaven. Jesus in the Garden of Gethsemane addressed him as 'Abba', the word which also may have begun the Lord's Prayer in Aramaic, but this may not be baby-talk. In spite of the interpretation found in the English Puritans and the work of the esteemed scholar of our time, Joachim Jeremias and retailed in innumerable sermons and popular addresses, it has been argued that it does not mean 'Daddy', but has 'the nuance of solemn and responsible adult speech'.[9] The father is also king. The central and controlling petition of the one prayer that Jesus taught his followers is 'Thy kingdom come'. Another meaning of that unusual word translated 'daily' in the petition for bread, would refer it to the kingdom, 'Give us today a foretaste of the heavenly feast in the kingdom'.

Jesus may well have hoped that the prayer he taught was to be answered in Gethsemane. The kingdom did not break in under that Paschal moon. The doing of the Father's heavenly will on earth meant that he must drain to the dregs the bitter cup of God's judgment on sin and unspeakable suffering. The gospel of the kingdom rather fades from the New Testament writings subsequent to the first three gospels, until we arrive at the Revelation of John, but Christians have continued to pray the Lord's prayer and are to live always with a sense of the kingdom's imminence. As Rudolph Otto wrote years ago:

The Kingdom is not kingly dignity and kingly rule, not a locality or a sovereign state, not a people or a community, but all these blended together. God's might and holiness and glory, and his throne and the power of his rule, and his angels and their ranks, and the blessed ones and saints at his throne, and the community of the righteous and the Church triumphant and the new heaven and earth, transfigured existence and heavenly blessedness and the life everlasting and 'God all in all' – all these belong here as a whole together. And this whole should someday 'come' and we should 'enter into it' (and when things are ordered aright, then we have in a manner a foretaste and anticipation, and in faith and rebirth we are 'actually' already therein). All this a Christian intends, and he prays about all this, whenever he prays: 'Thy Kingdom come'.[10]

Matthew and Luke both record a prayer of Jesus of exultant thanksgiving.[11] Luke says that he 'exulted in the Holy Spirit', a comparatively rare reference in the gospels to the one whom Christians have seen as the third person of the Trinity. There is a charismatic implication. The followers of Jesus have much cause for joy in the presence of the kingdom and the limitless grace of God, with its good news for the poor, its welcome for sinners and its 'undistinguishing regard' for helpless humanity. In the farewell discourses of the Fourth Gospel, there is promise of a joy in the Easter return of Jesus that no one can take away. The lyrical note is found in the whole of the New Testament and must have arisen from Jesus himself. Yet there is austerity and asceticism in his teaching. Discipleship means bearing a cross and renunciation of the dearest human bonds.[12] In Luke this is not the willingness to be crucified with Christ in the terrible crisis of his earthly ministry. The cross is to be taken up 'day after day'. There must be constant dying to self in Christian discipleship.

It has been suggested, though, that Jesus taught two ways of discipleship and that complete renunciation was not the vocation of all. J. C. O'Neill has put forward the idea that some of the teaching of the Synoptic Gospels presupposes a monastic community. Monasticism did not begin with a supposed protest against the worldliness of the church after Constantine had made Christianity the official religion of the Roman Empire. It was there from the start. Jewish monasticism had existed for a long time. The fiercer commands of Jesus and the New Testament are directed to this calling, celibate, communal, ascetic.

> I even wonder if Jesus did not give extensive particular instructions to those who were called to live the common life, instructions which were not meant to apply to all who believed. Perhaps much of the material in the Sermon on the Mount and the sermon on the Plain is drawn from this special body of teaching. The absence of most of this type of teaching may be no accident: Mark could well have been the collection of teaching and deeds meant for the church at large, people who went on marrying and having children and owning property.[13]

On the other hand, Stephen Barton, in his study of *The Spirituality of the Gospels*, sees Mark's as a 'dark, strenuous spirituality', a 'gospel of Passion from beginning to end' with little joy and no humour, only rather bitter irony.[14] One may dispute O'Neill's hypothesis there. Austin Farrer's syllogism may well get to the heart of Mark's Gospel:

> God gives everything.
> Give everything to God.
> YOU CAN'T!

But the notion of two ways may be pertinent to the teaching given to the intimate circle of disciples. The Sermon on the Mount is addressed to Jesus' disciples gathered around him. The crowds may not have followed him up the mountain. Yet much of his ministry, in the early days at any rate, was to the multitude, the sight of whom moved him with compassion, to whom he revealed God's power and mercy in his works of healing, from whom he called the socially ostracized and rejected. O'Neill wonders if the house of Levi's feast may not have been 'a settled refuge for converted sinners who have to learn to live the new life together, without possessions and power'.[15] Meanwhile, according to Mark 4.10ff., the majority are outside. They have to be content with parables which seem to darken counsel rather than make all things plain. There is irony here and sadness that so few understand. Yet some are able to receive the teaching to a certain extent. They may not understand as much as those called to enter into the mystery of the kingdom of God. But they are not totally without salvation and may be influenced in their lives by something of the divine grace, though they do not give themselves to the severities of total dedication, the 'massive heroism' of the few, or have that intimate knowledge of God which is given to some for the benefit of all. They are not exempt from those crosses which most have to bear in this transitory life – disease, accident, bereavement, hardship, handicap, financial ruin, natural or human disaster, dying – and these may, though not inevitably, bring them nearer to God.

Chapter 2

The Spirituality of the Early Church

The centre of the New Testament is the death of Jesus and its consequences. Apart from the letter of James it dominates the collection. The Gospel of Thomas, not in the New Testament, has no Passion story, while the Didache, a liturgy now believed to come from the late first, or early second century, has no explicit reference to the Lord's death. In those writings which the church has accepted as authoritative, the death of Jesus by crucifixion is the wellspring of spirituality. There is great restraint in describing the physical horrors of this terrible death. In the sparse description there is enough for the imagination of Christians to dwell on and mourn. The manner of death is of symbolic significance for Paul and John. But it is the death of Jesus more than the indescribable physical agonies that accompanied it which matters for the New Testament. Believers are identified with Christ's death in baptism which means a radical transfer from the life of sin to the life of grace.

The age of the Fathers

Most Christians have been brought up to picture the early Christian centuries as a continuation of the Acts of the Apostles – a glorious and triumphant expansion, with persecutions, until Christianity prevailed under Constantine at the beginning of the fourth century to become the official religion of the by then declining and soon to be divided Empire. Those of our time who are anti-establishment believe this was the beginning of a deterioration from which Christianity has never wholly recovered, though there have been saints and lovers of God, and prophetic rebels against the existing order, with whom the truth has usually lain.

This is far too simplistic. There were contentions from the first, not only with opponents of the gospel but among Christians themselves and many spiritualities flowed from the Christ-event, depending to some degree on secular milieux. Sects and parties abounded. The Christians were not as on the day of Pentecost 'all with one accord in one place'. There were Syrian ascetics following the lowly Jesus, 'poor and catching fish for dinner and supper, satisfying many thousands with a little bread, resting from the fatigue of a journey like a man, and walking on the waves of the sea like a God'.[1] There were those for whom Christianity was a new law, to whom the cross and redemption seem to have counted for little, and those for whom it was above all supernatural, signs and wonders and portents, increasingly spine chilling in its rites of initiation and eucharist as the first millennium rolled on. The faith of the cities was different from that of the countryside. And throughout the years, the church was feeling its way towards what became the orthodoxy of the fourth century and later creeds. From the end of the first century the baptismal formula of Matthew 28.20, the triple name of Father, Son and Holy Spirit, was customary, but the interpretations were in many cases far from the Trinitarianism of the fourth century, which spoke of 'three persons equally divine'. Both Son and Spirit were often seen as in some sense subordinate manifestations or powers of the one God. The doxology was 'Glory be to the Father, through the Son in the Holy Spirit'. In the end the theologians won through, as we see from their prominence as early as the New Testament itself. They exerted their influence by communication, by written correspondence and as emissaries; also, one would like to think, by the coherence and evident truth of their teaching, its foundational belief the possibility through Jesus Christ of a relationship between human beings and the mysterious yet manifest God who had made and sought them for himself. And it must be remembered that the early theologians were not academic professionals but pastors and bishops in daily association with the churches.

The 'peace of the church' under Constantine was a recognition of long-standing developments as the church accommodated itself to living in the world, or to use Marxist language, under 'the systems', which the Johannine writings of the New Testament so much deplore and regard as a realm alien to the life of God revealed in Christ. There was great opposition between church and society at first. Christianity was incompatible with much in society. There were many prohibited avocations. A Christian could not be a soldier. It is debated as to whether this was out of a belief in pacifism or because military service involved acknowledging the Emperor as divine. No Christian could be a gladiator or an actor, or a teacher where it was necessary to tell stories of the gods. Persecution may have been only intermittent, but that very fact created perpetual insecurity, since Christians never knew when it might break out with full atrocities. To be a Christian was a matter of life and death, and the possibility and prospect of martyrdom made Christ's second-century followers more than ever conscious of their crucified Lord, and of Christian discipleship as a dying life. As Ignatius of Antioch wrote in his letter to the Romans (c.110), 'For I who write to you am living, yet in love with death. My Love is crucified, and in me there is no earth-fed fire, but living water speaking in my heart and saying, Come hither to the Father.' (Scholars have differed as to whether 'my Love', in Greek *eros*, means Jesus himself, or 'this earthly part of me' my carnal appetites, human desires. Either way – and in different hymns Charles Wesley uses the phrase in both senses – death, for Ignatius, is the supreme and joyful union with the crucified Christ.)

Adventuring out of the Middle East into the Hellenistic world of Athens and Alexandria and so to Europe, the church was confronted by much religion, including the austere and ethical synagogues, spiritualizing the sacrifices once offered in the now destroyed Temple at Jerusalem, but also pagan cults, the confused and esoteric beliefs labelled 'Gnostic', and philosophically neo-Platonism, which also influenced Judaism. This last may be described simply as involving belief in the supremacy of mind over the passions.

The spiritual reading of Scripture

In answer to Judaism, Christianity did not abandon the Hebrew scriptures. One teacher, Marcion (died c.160), would have jettisoned all of these writings, and most of what came to be the New Testament too, because he felt it had been written under their influence. He retained ten of Paul's letters and an edited version of St Luke's Gospel. He contended that Christianity was a gospel of love not law and that the Jewish God of the Old Testament is a different being from the God and Father of Jesus Christ. He was condemned as a heretic. Justin Martyr in his Dialogue with the Jew Trypho (c.135) uses many arguments to convince his disputant that the old covenant has passed away now that Christ has come, that the Logos (Word), made flesh in Christ, has replaced the Old Testament God, just as Gentiles have replaced Jews as the chosen people.

Christians interpreted the Old Testament by means of allegory, a Jewish method constantly used by Paul (e.g., I Corinthians 10.1ff.; Galatians 4.23–31) and by most New Testament writers, but with which Marcion would have nothing to do. They also applied it to the Christian scriptures. They were not primarily concerned, as students of Scripture from the eighteenth century onwards have been, to establish what actually happened in history, though they would assume it in broad outline. They were mostly intent on edification and guidance for the present and future as the purpose of Scripture. Paul says this in effect in I Corinthians 10.11 with reference to the calamities and sufferings of Israel in the wilderness.

The history is written down not primarily to reconstruct what happened then, but in order that Christians may learn from it and, being warned, live better lives. Allegory was also a help in finding more than scandal and embarrassment in the unsavoury details of the Old Testament; and also in reconciling those passages which speak of God very much as a being with human feelings and senses, with the prophetic insistence that he is not such a one as ourselves and the metaphysical demand that he is pure Spirit.

The basis of allegory lies in the fact that a text is often susceptible of several meanings. The literal meaning may conceal the spiritual. It is not unimportant and is often historically true, but by itself may be a dead, if not killing letter. Preoccupation with it may prevent us from making that 'costing choice', that decision or resolve of faith which changes our whole life. And what above all else inspired the use of allegory for Christians was the belief that from beginning to end the Bible is a book about Jesus Christ. The risen Jesus himself, according to Luke 24, encouraged this belief and though he may have been selective – not every syllable referred to him – 'the Law of Moses and the Prophets and the Psalms' does comprehend the whole of Jewish sacred Scripture.[2] It is prophetic of his glory through suffering.

In John 3.14, the brazen serpent of Numbers 21.9 represents Christ lifted up, exalted on the cross. He is the Bread of Life, of which the manna in the wilderness was but the prefigurement in the vicissitudes of this moral vale. The Jewish Temple symbolizes his body of which Jonah's three days and nights in the whale's belly prophesy the interment in the depths of the earth from which he will be raised up. The letter to the Hebrews, with it Hellenistic influence, uses the liturgy of the Jewish tabernacle and the religion of the old covenant to proclaim the final and all-sufficient high priesthood of Christ. They are types and shadows of what has now been made plain through the divine Son.

Later Christians saw the patriarchs and priests as types of Christ. They believed that he was the mysterious Melchizedek,

King of Salem, priest of the most high God, who fed Abram, after his warfare, with bread and wine. This for many Christians has been an anticipation of the eucharist, though the letter to the Hebrews, puzzlingly for some, does not make this connection or mention the sacrament of all.[3] Christ it was who appeared awesomely to Joshua before Jericho, a drawn sword in his hand, as the captain of the Lord's host.[4] He was the mysterious fourth with the three in the fiery furnace.[5] Allegory may be far fetched. Some have seen the fusion of metals in the construction of the Temple as a type of the union of the three persons in the Godhead, or the red curtains of the tabernacle as a prophecy of Christ's blood. Babylon's babies to be dashed against the rock in vehement hatred still evident in tribal and other wars today, are 'my sins', the rock according to the Spanish Carmelite, John of the Cross, being Christ.[6] The Eastern Orthodox liturgy for the Annunciation has Ezekiel 44.1ff. as a lesson. The permanently shut eastern outer gate of the Temple is a type of Mary, the Lord's mother, God bearer, immaculate, intact, forever virgin. The coals which the Seraphim brought live from the altar to cleanse the prophet's lips in Isaiah 6 are Christ, borne in the tongs which are the virgin's womb. And allegory, in spite of its spiritual intent as against literalism, may fail to confront us with the demands of historical reality. It may smooth the roughness of the revelation, 'the old coarse gospel', which belongs not only to some universe of Platonic ideas, but to the world of fish and chips, bread, circuses, concentration camps and wars. There is also the fact, offensive to some, though others interpret it poetically and true to daily perceptions, that much allegory presupposes a three-tier universe. More seriously, the theology of the Fathers often seems to us childish, picturesque, and of a mythology of fall and redemption which does not seem to correspond to the universe as we know it, or seem true to our understanding of God-in-Christ. We like to think that our understanding is truer to the New Testament than the Fathers' interpretation, closer though they were in time.

Allegory has tended to be frowned on since the Second

World War, the period when higher criticism captured the intellectual heights. We no longer read the Bible in this way. Until then it had tremendous vogue. In the early third century, one of the greatest exponents of allegory, Origen, in his *Homilies on Leviticus*, 'gives a spiritual meaning to every detail of ceremonial worship, distinguishing for example the cases in which the sacrificial meat must be cooked in the oven, on the stove, or on the grill'.[7] Henri Crouzel points out that this was due to his belief, held in common with many of the ancient Fathers, that the Bible was dictated by the Holy Spirit, so that no word, no detail is useless and without spiritual meaning. Understanding Scripture was not simply 'an academic exercise but a religious experience'.[8] Centuries later, Charles Wesley, meditating on the words of Jesus in St Luke's Gospel, 'I have come to cast fire on the earth' (12.49), which he interpreted as the fire of divine love, not of judgment (though as T. S. Eliot saw, the two are both devised by love) immediately thought of Leviticus 6.13, 'the fire must always be kept burning on the altar, it must not go out'. And so he wrote the hymn:

> O Thou who camest from above
> The pure celestial fire to impart,
> Kindle a flame of sacred love
> On the mean altar of my heart!
>
> There let it for thy glory burn
> With inextinguishable blaze,
> And trembling to its source return,
> In humble prayer and fervent praise.
>
> Jesus, confirm my heart's desire
> To work and speak and think for thee;
> Still let me guard the holy fire,
> And still stir up thy gift in me;
>
> Ready for all thy perfect will,
> My acts of faith and love repeat,

> Till death thy endless mercies seal
> And make the sacrifice complete.

There is an allusion in the third verse to II Tim. 1.6, in the words of the Authorized Version, 'stir up the gift of God that is within thee', found in the Anglican order for the consecration of bishops. There could also be a reference to stirring the fire. Christians have allegorized the New Testament as well. Indeed, according to the Gospel writers the parables themselves are allegories, a view which having been discounted as the misguided interpretation of later preachers, has come back into fashion. No one has gone to greater lengths than the Western Father, Augustine (354–430) with his interpretation of the parable of the Good Samaritan, in which every detail has a meaning beyond the literal, derived from Christian mythology. To mention but a few: the man going down from Jerusalem to Jericho who falls among thieves is Adam: the thieves are the devil and his angels; the priest and the Levite who pass by on the other side are the ministers of the old covenant, helpless to save; the Samaritan, which means Guardian, is Christ; the beast is the flesh which Christ assumed and being set upon it is belief in the incarnation; the inn is the church: the innkeeper, Paul.

'The other side', referring in the gospels to the opposite shore of the sea of Galilee from most of Jesus' ministry, has been allegorized as the life beyond death, as in the words engraved on the Northamptonshire tombstone of an aged couple early in the twentieth century: 'At eventide, Jesus called them to the other side.'[9] There is also the Israelites crossing to the other side of Jordan, the Promised Land in Joshua 3.17, as in the third verse of William Williams' hymn 'Guide me O thou great Jehovah'.

> When I tread the verge of Jordan,
> Bid my anxious fears subside:
> Death of death and hell's Destruction,
> Land me safe on Canaan's side.

For most of the centuries Christians have lived in the scriptures in this way. Two outstanding preachers of the twentieth century have been allegorizers. Ronald Knox, best known as a Roman Catholic, stylist, wit and translator of the Bible, has a sermon on Ruth 2.8, in which Boaz tells Ruth 'Go not to glean in any other field'. Based on a book of French devotion the field of the sermon is the eucharist, the mass. Many today would say that a sermon on Ruth should deal rather with the treatment of aliens, or her constancy and support of Naomi. Her undoubted sex appeal may be muted, but above all is her woman's decisive place in the history from which Jesus came.

Kenneth Kirk, Oxford scholar, moral theologian and Anglo-Catholic leader, seems to have used allegory in most of his sermons. One of profound spiritual teaching is from Genesis 2.14, 'The fourth river is Euphrates', in which he begins with a piece of literary criticism which dilates on the skilled and sparing use of words by which great authors attain perfect economy of expression and then goes on to remark that while the writer of Genesis gives some description of the other three rivers which flow from Eden, he merely says of the last 'the greatest and most significant of them all', 'the fourth river is Euphrates'. This brusque sentence, noted incidentally by Augustine, marks a transition from romance to reality, from idealism to actual life. We must not 'linger too long upon the heights of idealistic day-dreaming', but 'put our aspirations to the test by applying them to the needs, problems and temptations of everyday life'. Yet drab and colourless Euphrates has its spring in the paradise of God. There should therefore be no disillusionment, no pessimism, no cynicism, but the vision with which the incarnation opens our eyes. Our realism must be accompanied by the awareness of grace all around us and our true citizenship in heaven. But there is also a trumpet call in these blunt words. 'The fourth river is Euphrates – *and that is evidence you cannot ignore*'. The daily life of the Christian should disprove all doubts about God and the unseen world. It will do so unselfconsciously. The saint will know that he has found the way, or rather that the way has found him, but he will not advertise himself, think of himself as a saint, or listen for others to acclaim him. He will labour to make his life more helpful to others and be properly self-critical without falling into the Slough of Despond. But he will hope and pray that the fourth river of his visible life 'will prove the reality of the three mystic rivers which men can see by faith alone'. The Euphrates of our daily life may seem to us 'a puny, sordid stream', but if our hearts are set on doing God's will, he may make of it 'a mighty river whose testimony to the power of his grace no one shall be able to gainsay'.[10]

Andrew Louth, in *Discerning the Mystery*, sought with wide learning to rehabilitate allegory. It is not incompatible with some of the latest literary criticism. The idea that there is one authentic 'original meaning' in a text, which allegory ignores or evades, is now challenged.

> . . . in interpreting a piece of writing it is not a matter of my attempting to reconstruct the original historical context in which it was written and thus to divine what was originally meant in an act of imagination, but rather a matter of listening to what was written, listening across a historical gulf which is not empty, however, but filled with the tradition that brings this piece of writing to me, and brings me not only that piece of writing but preconceptions and prejudices that enable me to pick up the resonances of the images and arguments used in whatever it is I am seeking to understand.[11]

The association of ideas and powers of recall are always present in our experience and our understanding and interpretation. They certainly affect our serious reading of Scripture in devotion and hearing of it in liturgy. A man of my generation – perhaps it is different for those who are younger – is bound to remember what certain texts meant to his father, as well as possessing through historical scholarship knowledge of exegesis of the past. All these are the close neighbours of allegory.

Louth's conclusion, following Augustine and Pascal, is that allegory helps us to discern a pattern in Scripture, and that it should be used not as an arsenal but as a treasury. Christianity is not the religion of the Book but of the Word, 'living and incarnate'. He quotes Henri de Lubac, Christianity is not 'the biblical religion: it is the religion of Jesus Christ'. So we are brought back to the belief that the key to the scriptures is the mystery of Christ, his cross, death, resurrection and faith in him. Or to put it another way, with Pascal, 'the sole object of Scripture is love'.[12]

Whether there will be a return to allegory in Christian spirituality is uncertain. It has great fascination and is a natural function of the human mind. The present flight from history and attempts to discover original meanings may encourage it, as well as techniques of Bible reading and meditation for which the question 'What does this say to me?' is central. I have told elsewhere[13] of the group of Christians in poverty-stricken circumstances in Brazil who read the story of the feeding of the five thousand, and asked what it called on them to do. They fastened onto the five loaves and two fishes and said 'Let five families in work look after two families unemployed!' They by-passed the main details of the story, its place in the gospels and its miracle, altogether. They were aware that at its basic level the story is about feeding the hungry and were not escaping into a supposed 'spiritual' world removed from their people's plight. C. F. D. Moule suggested to me that they might have decided on similar action had they been asking the same question of 'Green grow the rushes O!' But they were reading the story as Christians intent on Christian action in consequence. To a group from a different culture, in Oxford say, Kirk's sermon may have had a similar effect if the practical question had been raised. Allegory may be dangerously seductive unless it issues in resolve. And though we must not be enslaved by literalism, textual analysis and R. G. Collingwood's historian's 'torturing the evidence' remain the vocations of some who through the asceticism of scholarship are the allies not the enemies of spirituality.

Christian Platonists and prayer

It was vital for the early church that Christianity should be shown to be more than magic and old wives' tales, just as it should come to grips with the Gnostics, doubly dangerous because, like the New Age movement of our time, they took so much of Christianity into their systems. Among other things the Gnostics esteemed St Paul, which did not help his reputation in the second century and after.

It was in Alexandria from the second half of the second century that there arose the Catechetical school, which has been claimed as the noblest scheme of Christian education ever projected. With no buildings of its own, in learning it rivalled the university. Not uncritical of the Greek philosophers, it admired them, found links between Plato and Moses and sought to claim them for Christ. Its outstanding teachers were Clement (c.150–213) and Origen (185–254). Their spiritualities would never have divorced the spiritual and the intellectual, the philosophic and the missionary. Origen's theology was, in Henri Crouzel's words, 'a research theology'. He often made but modest claims for his ideas, and was willing to revise or surrender them in the light of better understanding of the living Word.

Clement, whose influence has been greater on posterity than in his own time, was more respectful to Plato than Origen. He believed that knowledge was the way of Christian perfection and called his ideal Christian the (Christian) Gnostic. The pursuit of knowledge is a religious duty. Knowledge and love are one. We can love only what we know, which implies the purgation of love from mere sensuality or eroticism. We may, with qualifications, apply the seventeenth-century Jewish philosopher, Spinoza's phrase to Clement and say that for him the goal was the intellectual love of God. But in total contrast to Spinoza, Clement would have endorsed the Johannine declaration 'we love because he first loved us'.

He first undertook the formation of a Christian doctrine of prayer. For him, as for so many others of the Fathers and indeed to a twentieth-century teacher such as W. R. Inge, Dean of St Paul's from 1911 to 1934, prayer is 'the ascent of the mind to God'. 'The mind was never for them the soulless instrument of mere discursive reasoning, of the naked logical or dialectical process.' It was able 'to uplift the whole spirit out of the tumult of passion', but in its search for truth, its supreme function, 'it carried of necessity the whole nature with it'.[14]

The implication of this is that all life is prayer. The apostolic injunction 'Pray without ceasing' is no counsel of impossibility amid the turmoil of the world:

> Holding festival in our whole life, persuaded that God is altogether on every side, we cultivate our fields praising: we sail the sea hymning, in all the rest of our conversation we conduct ourselves according to rule. The Gnostic then is very closely allied to God, being at once grave and cheerful in all things – grave on account of the bent of his soul towards the Divine, and cheerful on account of the consideration of the blessings of humanity which God has given us.[15]

'Conversation' does not mean simply talking, but the whole way of life and its relationships. Origen includes 'deeds of virtue or fulfilling the commandments' as parts of prayer. 'For the only way we can accept the commandment "pray constantly" (I Thess. 5.17) . . . is by saying that the entire life of the saint taken as a whole is a single great prayer. What is commonly called prayer, is then, a part of prayer.'[16]

Petition is not lacking in Clement, though it must be for those things which are in accordance with God's will and therefore which concern the soul. We do not ask for the necessities of life, and this in spite of petition for daily bread in the Lord's Prayer. This is totally different from the earlier Roman Cicero, who said that while it was right to pray to the gods for material benefits, virtue must be our own achievement else it would not be true virtue.

Origin insists that we 'must pray for the things that are chiefly and truly great and heavenly', but God will sometimes give us those corporeal benefits that pertain to them. We read in the Old Testament of how Hannah received her longed for child, Samuel, but this was in some sense a by-product of her being delivered from spiritual sterility. The material gifts are the shadows cast by the spiritual and just as in some latitudes sundials cast no shadows so they may be withheld, though at other times are long; but, no matter, for shadows are fleeting at best. Spiritual gifts are above all to be desired.[17]

In his commentary on the Lord's Prayer, Origen raids all Scripture for the interpretation of the prayer for daily bread and concludes that the bread requested is 'the living bread which comes down from heaven' of John 6. He does not make reference to the eucharistic bread. He remarks that the Greek word *epiousion* translated 'daily' is not in use either in learned or colloquial speech and must have been invented by the evangelists. He finds the root *ousia*, 'being', and translates as 'daily bread for our being'. It is to nourish us to immortality. It is the bread of angels and through it we may be made divine. Origen glances at what has become an interpretation favoured by some modern expositors that *epiousion* is derived from *epienai*, 'come upon' which means the bread of tomorrow, the coming kingdom, anticipated today, but he prefers his own interpretation.[18]

For both Clement and Origen the goal of the Christian life is the vision of God, as it had been for Irenaeus of Lyons earlier. Origen devised a doctrine of five spiritual senses corresponding to the physical senses. These enable the soul to discern between good and evil and, in the words of the modern Roman Catholic theologian, Hans Urs von Balthasar, 'can be developed and improved to an infinite delicacy and precision, so as to report to the soul more and more unerringly what is the will of God in every situation'.[19] But the doctrine also expresses the richness of contemplation for which visual imagery alone is not sufficient. In a comment on the Song of Songs 2.9 which describes by analogy several ways in which the beloved reveals himself, Origen lists the various New Testament images of Christ which he assumes 'to suit the several senses of the soul':

> He is called the true light, therefore, that the soul's eyes may have something to lighten them. He is the Word, so that her ears may have something to hear. Again, he is the Bread of Life, so that the soul's palate may have something to taste. And the same way, he is called spikenard or ointment, that the soul's sense of smell may apprehend the fragrance of the Word. For the same reason he is also said to be able to be felt and handled, and is called the Word made flesh so that the hand of the interior soul may touch concerning the Word of Life. But all these things are the One, Same Word of God, who adapts himself to the sundry tempers of prayer according to these several guises and so leaves none of the soul's faculties empty of his grace.[20]

Prayer is supremely contemplation, which is a life lived by a person. The Platonist term for the goal of contemplation, the vision of God, is *theoria*. This does not come by discursive meditation on the life of Jesus, as in the teaching which has had such vogue since the Reformation, both Catholic and Protestant. Not that the earthly events of the life of Jesus can be ignored. Jesus as the Word is the object of contemplation, not least as crucified. But the incarnation is only a stage in the ascent to God. Yet it is essential because contemplation involves a personal encounter and the final vision is not the result of human effort, but the divine mercy and grace. In his teaching, whatever was at times his personal practice, Origen asserts that prayer should never be addressed to Jesus, the Logos. It is 'a glorifying of God through Christ who is glorified with him'. Jesus himself, the divine Son, prayed on earth and prays in heaven. We pray with him, not to him. His prayer gathers up all human prayers and those of angels and the saints in light, who 'now made more perfect in life, are better able to pray with and for the church on earth, bearing the griefs and burdens of those still struggling in their pilgrimage'.[21]

Yet, not without paradox in view of the implications of prayer as a bearing of burdens, contemplation is possible only to those who have achieved the state of *apatheia*, the undistracted calm and peace of mind which follow the subduing of the passions. 'It is a state of soul where enemies cannot trouble, where anxiety cannot disturb, where the changes and chances of mortality do not shake, where the will is detached and unwavering because it is set upon God.'[22] The Jesus of the Farewell Discourses of the Fourth Gospel is its supreme exemplar. A problem for spirituality is that this Jesus, who has drawn so many to himself in holy love, is different from the Jesus of Gethsemane found in the Synoptic Gospels, upon whom came terror and dismay as he agonized beneath the Paschal moon. Origen is uncomfortable with Gethsemane. He finds it hard to believe that the perfect spiritual being will know the fear of death. There is conflict here in Origen between the Judaeo-Christian and the Platonist, as there is throughout the history of spirituality.

Clement and Origen both believe that there is no limit to what human co-operation with God by self-discipline and the pursuit of knowledge may do for the soul. Clement had the greater appreciation of nature; Origen believed that a true spirituality would transcend what is perceived by the senses. Clement sees in Christ the Word and Light whereas 'the Cross in all its wonder, its bounty, its power, is always before the eyes of Origen'. The death of Jesus redeems the whole cosmos. 'All creation groaning and travailing in sympathy with man's distress is soothed and strengthened and will be restored to perfect harmony, by Him, who in the blood of Jesus reconciles all things to Himself whether they be things in earth or things in heaven'.[23] Origen was condemned because he did not disavow the possibility of the devil being saved if he were not implacable in his opposition to God; but he never said that the devil 'the father of malice and perdition and of those who are excluded from the kingdom of God' would be saved as such. Origen cannot be called a universalist.

Both Clement and Origen are optimists of grace. They believe that Man is made, in the higher element of the soul, 'after-the-image' of God and this cannot be obliterated, though it be overlaid, by the free choice of evil. Recovered by Christ we may grow more into it through the imitation and following of God and Christ, until there is perfect union and we attain *theoria* and see the Father as the Son sees him and shine with his glory. Origen says that 'we are on the road to perfection, if straining forward to what lies ahead we forget what lies behind'.[24]

Towards the end of the next century, the Cappadocian Father, Gregory of Nyssa, implies that this itself is the state of perfection. In his 'Life of Moses' he writes:

This truly is the vision of God: never to be satisfied in the desire to see him. But one must always be looking at what he can see, rekindle his desire to see more. Thus, no limit would interrupt the growth in the ascent to God, since no limit to the Good can be found nor is the increasing desire of the Good brought to an end because it is satisfied.[25]

This understanding would certainly save teaching about Christian perfection from some of its aberrations and dangers. Perfection is dynamic rather than static. The perfect could never testify to the fact, confess to attainment, or believe perfection to be a state entered instantaneously.

Origen is the originator, with some scanty help from the New Testament, of a doctrine which most Protestants have come to abhor, that through contemplation the human mind may be made divine, in Rowan Williams' words, 'a perfect reflection back to God of his own inner rationality'. The Christian destiny is 'to become God in Jesus'.[26] The development of this will concern us later.

What also causes difficulty both for Protestants and for modern Christians is the dread of sexuality which pervades the thought of Origen and, even more, that of Gregory of Nyssa. They went to extremes to fight sexual temptation,

Origen possibly castrating himself in youth, and many throughout the centuries submitting to extreme measures to overcome
passion, for instance, standing naked for hours in the cold
water of wells or even the sea. Their fear is understandable
as all human history shows, not least the turmoil of sexual
passions and the terrible consequences of excess in our own
day. Yet all the Fathers seemed to find in this instinct the
primary source of sin, ignoring its positive and creative good.
Virginity is the ideal, the life of heavenly blessedness. For
Gregory, this is perfection. He is aware that marriage has
God's blessing in Scripture, but of all human affections desire
should be the first to be abandoned on the way to God. And
Gregory frighteningly depicts its evils. We cannot but feel that
this seriously limits the Fathers' value for spirituality, though
a greater enlightenment does not of itself remove the dangers
of sexuality, nor relief from harsh repression extinguish lust.

Monasticism

As we have seen monasticism may have its origins before
Christ and be implicit in his teaching. In the early Christian
centuries it did not arise simply from the desire to escape a
corrupt church in an evil world, but from the quest for perfection, as with St Antony pierced by the Gospel for the day, the
story of the Rich Young Ruler in Matthew 19.16ff., and the
words of Jesus, 'If you wish to be perfect, go, sell your possessions and give to the poor and you will have treasure in
heaven; then come and follow me'.

Monasticism was primarily a lay movement. It is wrong, to
see it as does the Methodist scholar, H. B. Workman, as 'the
protest of the lay spirit'.[27] The monks fled from ordination,
some because they felt that its worldly preoccupations might
destroy opportunities for contemplation, some out of humility,
since such a holy calling might carry with it the danger of
pride.[28] In the fourth century the solitaries of the Egyptian
desert numbered thousands. By its end, at centres such as
Scete, the monks assembled in the great church for worship

on Saturdays and Sundays, but on other days worshipped from a common act in their own cells. The writings of Clement and Origen circulated and Origen may be regarded as the intellectual founder of Christian monasticism, though he wrote before it became so large a movement. He is ascetic in his commentaries on Scripture and in the way of life he urged. Mary seated at the Lord's feet was his ideal and he envied the Baptist who 'departed into the desert where the air was purer, the sky more open and God more intimately nigh'. But some monks felt that he corrupted the simplicity of the Christian life with book learning. Books, after all, are property, the poor cannot afford them, while the interpretations they contain and their speculations may foster doubts. In any case Origen was tainted with heresy.

Evagrius of Pontus (died 399) was Origen's principal follower in the earlier decades of Christian monasticism. To him, Owen Chadwick has said, properly belongs the title 'father of our literature of spirituality'. He was the master of John Cassian (c.360–433), who 'set western monasticism on sane lines' and 'was the first guide to the contemplative ideal in the history of western thought'.[29]

Evagrius was condemned as a heretic by the General Council of Constantinople in 553, but that was too late to diminish his previous influence, though it affected the preservation and survival of his works thereafter. The main points of his teaching have been reconstructed:

1. The contemplative life is the ideal, but this is possible only if the state of *apatheia* is attained by war against the demons which would possess the soul. This led him to analyse the nature of temptation, particularly that which assailed monks. He originated the classification which has become known as the 'seven deadly sins', though for him there were eight and they were temptations rather than sins and in this order – greed, lust, avarice, melancholy, anger, accidie (boredom with the life of prayer), vainglory and pride. He has no truck with the idea, popular with some in our time, that anger may be a virtue. It 'troubles the mind and causes ruin to the state of

prayer'. These temptations may be fought and *apatheia* attained by psalm singing, the study of Scripture, manual work and patiently remaining in the cell.

2. When the soul is ready for contemplation there are two stages: natural contemplation, which itself has two aspects, contemplation of God's works in the creation and the ideas behind them; and the knowledge of God which is 'the ignorance that is inexhaustible' and yet the light which flows from the mystery of the Holy Trinity and not simply illumines the soul, but unites it to God so that knower and known are one. This is *theologia*, theology.

3. *Theologia* is the realm of prayer. 'For Evagrius prayer is not so much an activity as a state, not so much something that you do as something that you are'. He writes, 'The state of prayer is an impassible habit which snatches up the soul that loves wisdom to the intellectual heights by a most sublime love.' It is contemplation not ratiocination (reasoning things out). It is above mere thought, which involves multiplicity of notions, arguing with oneself about various concepts and judging between them. It demands the purity of the single heart and eye, and is the gift of God, of grace. It is the result of God's condescension.

4. There is no dark night of the soul in Evagrius and no ecstasy, which like Origen, he disparaged. Unlike the prevailing tradition in East and West, he does not travel the apophatic or negative way, which has as its most important stage, a saying of what God is not, the awareness of the total inadequacy of our concepts to understand or describe him. For Evagrius, unlimited ignorance is always yielding to knowledge.[30]

John Cassian was probably, though not certainly, born in the modern Dobrudja in the Balkans. As a youth, he entered a monastery near the cave of the Nativity in far away Bethlehem. But he encountered a monk from Egypt and was so impressed that he determined with his friend, Germanus, to visit Egypt, which he felt must be the home of sanctity. They departed under solemn vow to return speedily. This proved impossible and after some years and a great struggle with

conscience, they obtained release from the promise. In Egypt
Cassian believed that he was able to learn the way of 'perfection' as nowhere else. Here he came under the influence of
Evagrius. When thirty years later and in the West he wrote
two books, *The Institutes* or rules and *The Conferences*, or
collections of spiritual wisdom, for the benefit of communities
near Marseilles, it was Egyptian monasticism which he taught
as his ideal. In the latter work this took the form of the suppos-
edly remembered words of Egyptian teachers. Cassian had to
leave Egypt and is found in Constantinople at the beginning
of the fifth century being ordained deacon against his will.
The inference is that as a disciple of Origen through Evagrius,
he had to seek the protection of the sympathetic bishop John
Chrysostom against Coptic and other opposition. Chrysostom
was no diplomatist, aroused enmity, not least by his preferment
of Egyptian refugees and was condemned and deposed so that
Cassian and others fled to Rome. Here he became friends with
the future Pope Leo the Great, but he did not remain in Rome
for many years and took up residence in Gaul. The barbarians
were at the gates and the Mediterranean coast was refuge, but
a more likely explanation is that he wished to be under the
rule of Proculus, a bishop sympathetic to monasticism, which
was being increasingly assailed by pagans and less ascetic
Christians who encouraged city mobs to mock and impede
monks.

Cassian believed that the monastic life was apostolic. Mar-
vels and miracles accompanied it. Yet these he disparaged.
'They contribute nothing but astonishment and do not other-
wise instruct the reader in the life of holiness.'

There are two monastic vocations, that in community and
that of hermits. The latter is the ideal, the senior school as
against the kindergarten. But, though solitary, the hermitic life
is not isolated. As already mentioned, the cells were within a
limited area and their occupants met at least on Saturdays and
Sundays for communal worship.

Cassian sees community life as a preparation for the higher
life of the desert. He says that only perfect men should go

into the desert. This inevitably creates a dilemma, for who will ever claim to be perfect? Certainly not Cassian himself, and he knows well that the life of the hermit has its own peculiar temptations, not least to vainglory. In *The Institutes* he analyses the temptations after Evagrius in a treatment, digressive and disorderly as we have it, interspersed with anecdotes. Strict discipline is necessary. His counsels, though, are practical and full of common sense. The monks' garb will be different in the climate of the south of France from that of Egypt. He prescribes it with each item given a spiritual meaning. The girdle has precedents in the prophets and apostles of Scripture. It signifies readiness and urgency. The monks' dress will be no more ostentatiously austere than it will be decorative. Similarly food will be plain and without elaboration, but it should nourish and strengthen. Fasting and abstinence must not be sources of pride. The postulant should spend at least a year in the guest house before he joins the full community. The worship will be so ordered that there is no unnecessary interruption of private prayer, no avoidance of manual work, which is necessary among other things, to conquer accidie. Cassian does not seem to have favoured scholarship, the labour of the mind, for this should be devoted entirely to prayer.[31]

Two of the *Conferences* are on the subject of prayer and attributed to an Egyptian teacher Abba Isaac. They are seminal for the monastic life, but even more for the Christian understanding of prayer, even though there may be that in them which repels Protestants, Evangelicals and Liberals.

The belief, not taught by Jesus or wholly true to human experience, that there are lower and higher levels of prayer derives from Cassian. With his Platonist doctrine of the supremacy of mind, he is troubled by the mind's 'mobility'. Thoughts enter it in swarms, yet to empty it is to leave it swept and garnished for demons or worse than worst and most degrading thoughts, for in its natural state these are accompanied by good. Control is essential until 'ascending' thoughts predominate and, at last, the mind is fixed on God alone. This is far beyond the prayer of petition, penitence, intercession. It is sometimes called 'fire prayer', for it leaps out towards God like a tongue of flame. The imagination is banished. As a quotation from St Antony puts it: 'It is not a perfect prayer in which the monk is conscious of himself or understands his prayer.'

Yet Scripture underlies it and in particular the Psalms, which in Cassian assume for the first time the place they have continued to hold in Christian worship. Especially important for him is the verse that became the versicle and response at the opening of the offices (or 'duties' of regular worship), omitted from some modern revisions, 'O God make speed to save me: O Lord make haste to help me':

Whatever work you do, or office you hold, or journey you go, sing this verse while you are doing it . . . This thought in the heart may be a saving formula. It can ward off the demons. It can purify you from sin and earthly stain, and lead you to contemplate the heaven which eyes cannot see, and carry you upward to that ineffable prayer of fire which so few have experienced. Meditate upon the verse as you fall asleep; let it so mould your mind that it is the thought of your sleeping hours. When you wake let it be the first thought of your mind and let it send you down to your knees and then go forth with you to your day's work.

It is easy to see how this developed into the eastern hesychasm, roughly translated, 'the prayer of quiet', which has been most notably achieved by use of the Jesus Prayer, 'Lord Jesus Christ, Son of God have mercy upon me (a sinner)', often accompanied by control of the breathing.

Although the goal is the vision of God, not perfectly attained in this life, anticipated here below in a state of unselfconscious fixation of the mind on God alone, Cassian seems to qualify the more extreme statements about this when he describes, eloquently, the different ways in which we contemplate God:

He is seen in the grandeur of his created work. He is seen when we meditate upon his justice, or the daily gift of grace; or when we consider what he has done through his saints in their several generations; when we marvel and tremble at the power which guides the universe, or the eye which sees the secret of all hearts; when we remember that he numbers the sands and the waves and the raindrops, and that all time, past and future, is present to his mind; when we gaze in a kind of ecstasy at his unspeakable mercy with sinners; when we think upon his call which he bestowed upon us though we were unworthy, or upon the blessing of salvation given to them he has chosen, or how he brought us into the world and gave us his grace and the knowledge of his law even from our cradles; how he conquered the enemy; how he asks only for a good will and rewards us with eternal blessedness; how he was made man for our salvation; and gave his wonderful sacraments to the world.

The vision of God is union with him, though not absorption in the infinite and a loss of personal identity. It is a union of wills. It is a share in the life and love of the Blessed Trinity, a state

> ... where God shall be all our love and every desire and effort, every thought of ours, and all our life and words and breath and that unity which already exists between the Father and the Son, and the Son and the Father, has been shed abroad in our hearts and minds.

What must be emphasized is that this is attained through ceaseless meditation on Scripture. No more than for Origen is Christianity a Jesus cult and one must rise above contemplation of the incarnate life to the glorified Christ, not known any longer 'after the flesh'. Yet he is the same Jesus Christ and the monk can never forego his need of him.

The Rule of St Benedict

Cassian's works, advices rather than directives, are the source of the all-prevailing Rule of St Benedict, realistic, tolerant, wise, with a deep knowledge of human nature. Benedict, like the Cappadocian Father, Basil (died 379), was less entranced with Egypt, more concerned with the communal life than that of hermits and we may say, with the second great commandment of Jesus – love of neighbour. Basil devised Rules for monks and the seventh, 'if you always live alone whose feet will you wash?' is famous. Basil's monks lived in community, wore special garb, fasted and practised mortification. 'But they intended to serve the Churches. They administered relief to the poor, conducted a hospital and settlement for lepers, visited the sick, kept school'.[32]

There was always tension in monasticism between the communal and the solitary and between the quest for perfection, which could result in inhuman austerities and the realism, so manifest in the Rule of St Benedict as in Cassian. This might lead to compromise with the world. Corruption attacked all religious orders as they sought impossible ideals or compromised with the need to survive and establish themselves in time and place, or grew prosperous through regular work and good husbandry. No institutions were so much in need of perpetual reformation.

The influence of Monasticism on Christian spirituality is incalculable. We have seen this in the understanding of prayer. 'It established firmly and with a practical permanence the spiritual conditions and principles which must always regulate men's attempts to live in communion with God.'[33] To this must be added the keeping of hours with offices, or duties of worship, which became uniform or canonical under the Benedictine rule of eight daily offices in conformity with Psalm 119: 'Seven times each day I praise you' and 'at midnight I rise to give you thanks'. These daily offices were dominated by the Psalms. By the time of Benedict the whole Psalter was to be recited every week, a development of Cassian's recommendations. This was very different from the Jewish use and that of some early monasticism where the Psalter was more like a hymn book from which appropriate selections were to be made to suit occasions. The *Book of Common Prayer* reduced the eight offices to two – morning and evening prayer – and the Psalter was recited once a month, which is still the Anglican custom, though *Celebrating Common Prayer* (1992), a version of the daily office of the Society of St Francis, which increases the offices by adding Midday and Night Prayer, has various tables with different options for the use of the Psalms.

The Psalms

There is division of opinion as to the value and use of Psalms in Christian spirituality today. There is a renewed interest and a belief among some that they are indispensable, that they speak from ages past to a human condition that is perennial. This has been the feeling of Christians from Augustine to the Scottish Covenanters. It was not so apparent in the 1960s and the abandonment of Morning Prayer on Sundays in many English parish churches and the reduction of the number of Psalms at Sunday Evensong to one, means that Anglican Sunday worshippers are often deprived of them, while they do not seem often to be sung in Methodist worship, though they may be used as antiphonal readings. The *Alternative Service Book* of 1980, like the Roman Missal, provides for a Psalm between the Old and New Testament readings or as a gradual. Often a key verse is singled out as a refrain.

Should the whole Psalter be recited, cursing Psalms included, and those verses which John Wesley said were 'highly improper for the mouths of a Christian congregation'? In 1962, in a fine essay on Christian Prayer, the late Professor John Burnaby – author of *Amor Dei*, a study of Augustine's spirituality and one of the great books of the twentieth century (of which more later), is critical of much traditional liturgy as corresponding 'but ill to the essential character of Christian prayer' – if that character is best seen in the great saying of

St Paul, that 'God has sent into our hearts the Spirit of his Son, crying Abba Father'.[34]

> Of this incongruity, the Psalter, taken over as it stands from the worship of the pre-Christian synagogue, is the most conspicuous example. The Psalter owes its place in the Church's liturgy primarily to the ease with which it lent itself to interpretation by the early Church as prophetic of Christ. It has established its hold by the supreme beauty and truth of many of the Hebrew hymns and prayers which it contains. But the type of *Klage-Lied* of complaint or expostulation, to which not less than a quarter of the Psalms belong, is animated by a temper which not even the most reckless allegorising can scarcely baptise into Christianity. The authors of these Psalms are no less sure of their own piety than of the power of the God on whom that piety makes its demands. They are the 'righteous poor', oppressed and downtrodden by the godless and prosperous, the self-conscious 'saints' crying to God for vengeance upon their enemies.[35]

On the other hand, Dietrich Bonhoeffer, in the midst of Nazi persecution, insisted that the Psalms be used daily in private devotions if not in the congregation. 'St Jerome tells us that in his day people could be heard singing the Psalms in their fields and gardens. The Psalter filled the life of early Christendom. But what is more important, Jesus died on the Cross with words from the Psalms on his lips.'[36] This, however, could justify selection. Bonhoeffer will have none of it for it shows lack of reverence for the Bible's Prayer Book and is going one better than God. His approach is Lutheran and might, in part, have sounded strange to Cassian and Benedict. He reads the Psalter as the prayer of Christ. In its words we are joining our prayers to his. He puts himself completely in our place, prays for our forgiveness, while protestations of our innocence, offensive to Burnaby, affirm that, sinners though we are, we may plead his righteousness as justified believers.

Jesu, thy blood and righteousness
My beauty are, my glorious dress
Midst flaming worlds in these arrayed
With joy shall I lift up my head.

In spite of our remaining faults, we are in Christ innocent before God's enemies and before God himself.

Even Bonhoeffer finds 'the cursing psalms' a problem for Christians. They are not expressions of a personal quarrel or a taking of vengeance into our own hands. They are appeals to the justice of God, and, one may add, there is something wrong with a Christian who, in Bonhoeffer's age and ours, does not (contrary to Evagrius and *apatheia*) become vehement in face of the wickedness of the world, its unspeakable and not decreasing horrors and cruelties. And we ourselves are under the judgment of God. The mystery for Bonhoeffer and his master Luther, is that the divine vengeance for which the Psalmists pray fell on God's own Son. He himself suffered the wrath of God against sinners. 'God hates and condemns his enemies in the only just One, and this just One prays for their forgiveness.' 'So the cursing Psalm leads to the cross of Christ and God's forgiving love of his enemies.' The imprecatory prayer has been mysteriously answered in Christ. Vengeance, which is God's alone, has been taken on Christ in the place of sinners and transformed into grace and joy and salvation for all.[37]

This is not a theology which, in spite of the vogue of Bonhoeffer, and 'Christianity without religion' has much appeal to those for whom the love of God is all and the cross of Christ understood chiefly as its supreme and cosmic revelation. Bonhoeffer's attitude to the Psalms is compatible with his insistence that the Christian vocation is not to strive for sanctity or be an example of faith, but to kneel beside Christ in Gethsemane and share his cry of forsakenness from the cross. And the issue of the Roman Catholic journal *Concilium* for June 1990 carries a piece, not without Bonhoeffer's influence, which would not deprive Christian spirituality of the cursing psalms. Here 'the poor and the oppressed denounce their historical ills, asking God to do justice by abstaining from doing justice themselves'. The author, Enzo Bianchi, head of an Italian ecumenical monastic community, sees in these Psalms a prayer which renounces human violence for divine intervention, while it accompanies 'human action and commitment in history'.[38]

Monastic influence on spirituality has had its disadvantages and constrictions. Though it proclaimed the gospel challenge to seek perfection, and was a spirituality for eagles and not simply for sparrows, its concept of two standards restricted the possibilities of worldly holiness. It took over the daily offices, which had begun in the corporate prayer of churches and made them less suitable as vehicles for the sanctification of time outside the cloister and, in the words of the Orthodox liturgical theologian, Alexander Schmemann, it 'privatized' prayer. 'Pray without ceasing' was the aim and Benedictine the maxim 'to pray is to work and to work is to pray', but much of the work, the weaving of baskets, the making of rope, had no significance in itself. It was not a vocation, but a means of prayer and a support for it. 'This is not an illumination of life and work by prayer, nor a joining of these things in prayer, not even a turning of life into prayer, but prayer as life, or, more properly the replacement of life by prayer.'[39] To some extent, the offices displaced the eucharist as the chief expression of corporate worship and the latter became an act of ascetic piety to help individuals in the warfare against demons rather than the joyful celebration of what God had done in Christ and of entry into the kingdom.

Augustine

Augustine (354–430) is the most influential of all the theologians of the Christian West. His theology is a synthesis of Greek and biblical thought, but, more importantly, it is enriched by philosophy and his amazing intellectual powers, born of his own psyche and experience. He had an overwhelming awareness of beauty and a longing for God, the Beauty, 'so old and so new'. This he had sought for years through the indulgence of his sensual nature in the lovely things of creation, which, though they exist in God, kept him from God. In the end it seemed as though it was God himself who intervened directly in his life, brought him to the faith of the scriptures after years of intellectual quest and experiments with several systems of belief, though always attended by the prayers of his Christian mother Monica. After practising at home and in Carthage, this North African teacher of rhetoric proceeded via Rome to Milan where the western Emperor had his court. There, in order to further his career by a wife's dowry, he put away the concubine with whom he had lived faithfully for fifteen years, though it was a purely physical relationship with no intellectual companionship. There was a son, Adeodatus, unwanted at first but soon to be dearly loved, an able boy, who was to die at seventeen. Milan offered not merely the lure of professional advance and of Platonic philosophy, which had lasting influence on him, but the preaching of the bishop, Ambrose, whose Christian proclamation satisfied Augustine's searchings. His quest culminated in the garden of the house in which he was lodging. In a turmoil of spirit almost a frenzy, he went into the garden to be alone, although a friend followed him. He was racked by temptations to incontinence almost to the point of ending his life, when he heard a child's voice repeating over and over again 'Pick up and read, pick up and read'. This seemed a divine command. He remembered Antony and the Gospel reading. He hastened to where he had left a copy of the Letter to the Romans, opened it and his eyes lit on the words, 'Not in riots and drunken parties, not in eroticism and indecencies, not in strife and rivalry, but put on the Lord Jesus Christ and make no provision for the flesh and its lusts'.[40] 'At once with the last words of this sentence, it was as if a light of relief from all anxiety flooded into my heart. All the shadows of doubt were dispelled.'[41]

This was all the working of the mysterious Providence of God. Augustine's human will, his own efforts, would never have made him a Christian. He did not deserve the mercy of God. He had chosen to resist and exulted in his disobedience. All was of grace. And so Augustine declared 'My entire hope is exclusively in your very great mercy ... You command continence; grant what you command and command what you will'.[42]

This statement shocked a British monk, Pelagius, when he heard it quoted by a bishop who appeared to use it to condone sexual misdemeanours, and so began a bitter controversy which flared every now and then throughout the centuries, especially in the years after the Reformation and in the time of the Wesleys. Is the consequence of Augustine's doctrine, the question which so horrified St Paul – 'Shall we continue in sin that grace may abound?' – leading to antinomianism, the belief that Christians do not live by moral standards at all? Or if that extreme be denied is not the conclusion that what is required is the passivity of a faith which abandons all to God and does not strive towards perfection? Augustine's opponents caricatured his theology in some statements which accused him of teaching that God has created the greater part of the human race for eternal damnation, that God is therefore the author of our sins and that the prayer 'Thy will be done' is for most people a prayer for damnation.

In the end Augustine rested all on the inscrutability of God whose grace had saved him, the totally undeserving. He believed in the ultimate divine justice in spite of the fact that only a few were saved and these not the righteous but sinners. He took refuge with St Paul in Romans 11.33 (Authorized Version), 'O the depth both of the wisdom and knowledge of God! how unsearchable are his judgments and his ways past finding out!'

Cassian opposed Augustine because the monastic experience rested on the co-operation of the human will and the divine grace. Cassian also used Romans 11.33 but differently from Augustine, rather as a warning that we must not probe into God's purposes by human reason. Theologically agnostic at this point, we realize the necessity for the right direction of the will through mortification (the killing of the evil tendencies in our nature), discipline and the life of prayer.

Augustine in his spiritual autobiography, the *Confessions*, addresses the record of his life and his theology to God. He muses and speculates and questions before God. All is turned into prayer and is at once the confession of God's mercy and of his own sin. It has been said that he 'gossips with God' as no neo-Platonist would. In some ways it is the prototype of spontaneous, extempore prayer, the antecedent of later prayer meetings in chapels and homes, as when Augustine says 'I wrote *On the Beautiful and Fitting* in two or three books, I think – you know, O God, for I have forgotten'.[43]

The *Confessions* represents a new genre of writing which searches not only for meaning in a life but for identity of the subject. 'Where was I when I was seeking for you? You were there before me but I had departed from myself. I could not even find myself much less you.'[44]

There is poetry here which may not all be lost in translation, though its full artistry demands the original Latin. A professional orator, Augustine must speak to God with all the eloquence and beauty of language he can command, though art never displays itself at the expense of devotion. He is no longer repelled by what seems to a rhetorician to be the humble indeed crude, language of the Bible. The Psalms bind the *Confessions* together.

Here is one who hungers and thirsts for God and who knows no rest except in the divine love. This love is possible only through the mediatorship of Jesus Christ, the Word made flesh, who sits at God's right hand and intercedes with God for us. Herein is the only hope for sinners. 'We might have thought your Word was far removed from being united to mankind and have despaired of our lot unless he had become flesh and dwelt among us.'[45]

Augustine had a genius for friendship. He was tempted in his despair of himself to become a hermit, but this was not God's will or way for him. It was not just temperament but the incarnation which saved him from escaping to a solitude

in acknowledgement of the impassable gulf that stretched
between himself and God – '. . . you forbade me and comforted
me saying: "That is why Christ died for all, so that those who
live should not live for themselves but for him who died for
them".'[46] On his return to North Africa after his conversion,
he organized a lay community at his birthplace, Thagaste, on
quasi-monastic lines. He had to leave this when he became,
like Cassian and others, a somewhat reluctant ordinand, though
convinced that the people's clamour that he be made presbyter
was indeed the voice of God. But, earlier, the mystical vision
he had experienced at Ostia was shared with his mother,
Monica, just before her death. It is, says Henry Chadwick,
'perhaps a unique instance of a mystical experience for two,
simultaneously'. It is personal but not solitary. Andrew Louth
finds here 'a new note in monasticism, though it strikes a
chord that echoes back through the Hellenic – particularly the
Platonist – tradition to the group that gathered around Socrates
at the end of the fifth century BC'.[47]

It is not unexpected therefore that at the heart of Augustine's
spirituality should be the belief that God is Trinity. And that
man, made in God's image is trinity too – mind, knowledge
and love. He also finds three spiritual properties in the human
mind – memory, understanding and will. This which is the
source of self-love is also the evidence of the soul's capacity
to love God, to attain the wisdom that is above knowledge, to
be formed within itself into the image of the Trinity. Yet this
wisdom is not attainable in this life. 'Conversion does not
signify an end to the chaos of human experience.'[48] It mysteriously and unconsciously changes the influences which determine a life and the milieu of the soul. For Augustine, as
for Gregory of Nyssa, the Christian life is a never-ceasing
pilgrimage of the soul. As he says of his treatment of the
Psalms in the Latin version of the Vulgate, 'the only way you
can be perfect in this life is by knowing that you cannot be
perfect in this life'. He is cautious about *apatheia*, for emotion
is necessary to the fullness of human nature. The Christian
life is a cry 'out of the depths' (Psalm 130). Yet there is

advance, a journey to the heart's true home – language which has echoes of the neo-Platonist Plotinus – but it is a journey we could not make had not the Way itself come down to us.[49] This conquers the rhetorician's and the philosopher's pride:

> Build for yourself no other road for the attainment and possession of the truth than that which has been built by him who saw as God the weakness of our walking. And that is first humility, second humility, third humility . . . Not that there are no other commandments to be named; but unless humility precedes, accompanies and follows all our good actions, unless humility be set before us for our beholding, beside us for our adherence, over us for our restraint, then all the good of our joy in any attainment is wrested from us by pride.[50]

Augustine is cautious in his use of the language of deification. He prefers the more scriptural terminology of adoptive sonship. 'Out of sons of men he makes sons of God because out of the Son of God he made a Son of Man . . . and this is our promise of a share in his divinity. "Deification" is conferred by the identification of the believer in baptism with the Divine Son, whose own sonship is manifested in death and resurrection; it is not attained by a private flight of the alone to the alone.'[51]

The contemplative life was the ideal with which Augustine began his Christian course and he never relinquished it, but he came to see, as Burnaby makes clear, that all Christians are called to live successively the two lives of action and contemplation.

Allegorist as ever, Augustine sees these as typified by the two wives of Jacob – Leah and Rachel: 'The one temporal in which we labour, the other eternal in which we shall contemplate the fair beauty of God', though he does not reserve the latter entirely for the life of the world to come. Later and most intriguingly, he compares the Synoptic Gospels and John to 'the two virtues offered to man's soul, the one active, the other contemplative, the one by which we journey, the other which

brings us to journey's end'. In this life we attain the latter by
faith, which gives us a certain vision, through a glass darkly,
of unchanging truth. Like St Paul in II Corinthians 12, he
knows something of mystic rapture, being transported to the
third heaven, but he has come more to glory in his infirmities
which thrust him back on the grace of God.

Nevertheless, he sees the two lives illustrated in Peter and
John, and, of course, in Martha and Mary. 'Peter is called
loving rather than beloved; for we know our present trouble
and so must needs love the Saviour who delivers us from it,
whereas the Lord's love for us is less manifest in our trouble
than in our joy. John is beloved rather than loving; because
we as yet know not and possess not that contemplation of
truth wherein true joy is given to us.' Contemplation, like the
beloved disciple, may tarry till Christ comes and is made
perfect when he comes.

As for the two sisters, he realizes that Mary, hanging on
each word of Jesus, is like the congregation at worship. At a
time when there have been strong influences in Christianity
which demean sermons, it is well to be reminded that Mary
at Bethany was above all a good listener. But Augustine's
chief emphasis is on Mary's part that shall not be taken away.
There will be a time when ministering to need will no longer
be necessary. Many virtues dependent on the relief of distress
and those social services to the least which Christ in Matthew
25 says are done to him, will disappear as the saints near
journey's end. Meanwhile action is the servant of contemplation, the means to its end.[52]

Augustine was musical. He lived at a time, repeated in
church history, when there was controversy as to whether
music was permissible in worship and, if so, what kind it
should be. He himself was often moved to tears by it, his love
of God inflamed, but wondered whether this was not a sensual
excitement and self-indulgence, inimical to the Christian pilgrimage. He opined that, on balance, the custom of singing in
church was to be approved, though the music must not move
the hearer more than the subject of the song.[53]

He realized that music transcended speech, expressed those
emotions beyond the power of words. Preaching on the Psalms,
which he regarded as hymns of praise, he recalls workers
singing in the hot fields, who lose words and simply 'jubilate'.
He is commenting on the 'Jubilate', our Psalm 100.

There is a remarkable passage in his comment on the words
of Psalm 149.3: 'Let them sing praises unto him with tabret
and harp.' He points out that on a tambourine you have a
skin stretched out and in a stringed instrument catgut is
stretched out. In both instruments ordinary flesh is being
crucified.

> The man who said 'The world is crucified to me and I to
> the world' (Gal. 6.14) must have sung praises really well
> on this 'tabret and harp'! And he who loves a new song
> wants you to be that harp, that tabret.

So Paul strained, stretched forward to the goal, 'the prize of the
upward call'. So he stretched himself out, Christ touched him,
and 'the sweetness of the truth gave tongue'. So may it be for
us.

Rowan Williams points out the similarity between this and
one of George Herbert's Easter poems written over a thousand
years later:

> Awake my lute, and struggle for thy part
> > With all thy art,
>
> The cross taught all wood to resound his name,
> > Who bore the same.
>
> His stretched sinews taught all strings, what key
> Is best to celebrate this most high day.[54]

Augustine, like Origen, developed the notion of five spiritual
senses corresponding to the five physical means of loving
God:

When I love you what do I love? It is not physical beauty nor temporal glory nor the brightness of light dear to earthly eyes, nor the sweet melodies of all kinds of songs, nor the gentle odour of flowers and ointments and perfumes, not manna, or honey, nor limbs welcoming the embraces of the flesh; it is not these I love when I love my God. Yet there is a light I love, and a food, and a kind of embrace when I love my God – a light, voice, odour, food, embrace my inner man, where my soul is floodlit by light which space cannot contain, where there is a sound that time cannot seize, where there is a perfume which no breeze disperses, where there is a taste for food no amount of eating can lessen and where there is a bond of union that no satiety can part. That is what I love when I love my God.[55]

Some have objected that because Augustine maintains that the love of God is the true love of self, his spirituality is fundamentally self-centred. He points out, for instance, that the petitions of the Lord's Prayer are for oneself, but he is not simply an individualist. Community is one of the attributes of God who is Trinity. The Holy Spirit is the bond of love between the Father and the Son. In the very being of God love is possessed by being shared and this is so for us also, made as we are in God's image. Hence the necessity of the church, the sacrament of divine love, in which love is shared.

In the *Confessions* is the famous story of Victorinus, a septuagenarian orator and exponent of high culture with its 'gods many and lords many'. After reading Scripture and other Christian books, he declared himself a Christian. Simplicianus, Ambrose's father-in-God and baptizer, would not believe it until he had seen Victorinus in church. Victorinus retorted, laughingly, 'Then do walls make Christians?' In the end he accepted baptism, and was not ashamed of the mysteries of the humility of God's Word and the common life of all sorts and conditions in the Body of Christ.

The unity of the Church is the only safeguard of Christian love. Augustine uses the Latin word *caritas* or charity. He became dogmatic about this because while he was Bishop of Hippo. North Africa was torn by the Donatist schism, a fratricidal conflict, accompanied by terrorism and violence worthy of the IRA and the Ulster Loyalists, which in the end made him forswear the tolerance of his nature. Basic to his teaching is the word of Christ to Saul on the Damascus road, identifying himself with suffering Christians, 'Why persecutest thou me?' Augustine also finds the truth in the Farewell Discourses of the Fourth Gospel. Christ and his church are one. He says, 'We have been made not Christians only but Christ.' 'So' comments John Burnaby 'it is literally true that no Christian can call his soul his own; all who believe have one heart and one soul or life, the single life of Christ.'[56]

To sum up. Augustine's spirituality is a synthesis. The love of God is both *agape*, God's love for sinners, and *eros*, desire, which God also knows, since he has made us for himself. Deeply emotional and no disparager of feelings, Augustine is yet an intellectual: 'The ascent to God is a mental as well as an affective and emotional journey.'[57] Above all, in the words of Friedrich Heiler:

His religious thought and experience shows the most splendid synthesis of the Hellenistic concentration on the mystic search for the infinite and the biblical prophetic religion of revelation. In his praying are united the most profound contemplation and the most energetic strength of will, the passionate power of the biblical psalms and the serene depth of neo-Platonic absorption, Paul's faith in forgiving grace struggling out of the deep sense of guilt and the mystical Eros of Plato and Plotinus hastening heavenwards; the unconquerable trust in the divine will revealed in the Bible and the blissful contemplation of the neo-Platonic *summum bonum*. His praying is the expression both of the deep woe and weal of the heart and of the elevation of the mind to the Highest Good, of the humble cry to God 'out of the depths' and of the experience of essential oneness with God in his inmost soul.[58]

I would, however, question Heiler's opinion, which is not his alone, that neo-Platonic mysticism has precedence for Augustine. He has his moments of contemplative exaltation but these do not represent his ideal of Christian life in the world. The incarnation is paramount.

There have been those who have questioned Augustine's dominance in Christian spirituality. The Cambridge Platonists in seventeenth-century England repudiated the Augustinian tradition and approved only the neo-Platonist strain in him, while some in our own day feel he marks as serious a departure from authentic Christianity as Constantine does in the political sphere. It is his realism as well as his ardent love of God which accounts in part for his influence. He could not be optimistic either about human nature or human society, for he knew his own propensity to sin and lived in the declining years of the Roman Empire when the barbarians were at the gates and the dark ages loomed. This has seemed to many Christian thinkers to be the perpetual condition of humanity with transitory intervals of peace and prosperity in some civilizations at some periods. The City of God cannot be realized in history but is beyond time which, according to Augustine, was created with the world. In this world we have the church, necessary to Christianity both in its vocation as the community of love and its guardianship of the truth. It is a mixed community, though in it we anticipate the social joys of heaven:

> There we shall rest and we shall see; we shall see and we shall love, we shall love and we shall praise. Behold what shall be in the end without end.[59]

But, as the later hymn has it:

> Here we watch and struggle
> And here we live in hope
> And Zion in her anguish,
> With Babylon must cope.

The unity of the church in the true Catholic faith must be preserved at all costs.

Augustine opposed the extravagant hopes of millenarians and those who looked to an age of the Holy Spirit. There was to be no fulfilment in time. The focus of our hope was in the past, the once-for-all unique event of the incarnation, which contained our assurance of God's love, salvation. He suspected futurism and those notions, weird to the philosophic mind, of corybantic enthusiasm and the end of the age with the return of Christ who might be a new Messiah. These notions have recurred throughout history, as we shall see. They have some-times been savagely repressed by the orthodox and have never held Christian minds for long. But they do not go away totally. There are those in our time who feel they deserve more serious consideration than they have received with their Pentecostal faith, their practice of equality between the sexes and their gospel of hope for this world. Such people, like exponents of creation spirituality and original bliss rather than original sin, feel that Augustine's legacy has been a disastrous diversion, at least from the Acts of the Apostles. As was mentioned earlier, one does wonder with Augustine, as with all the Fathers, whether their sex obsession did not lead to a misunder-standing of sin. These matters will concern us more fully when we come to think of a spirituality for our confused times. Meanwhile Augustine's spirituality rises before us with the grandeur of some great cathedral. It is an edifice in whose richness many will find a home, and though, in spite of its spaciousness, some might see it as a prison, its foundation is God's love.

Chapter 3

The Medieval West

The spirituality of Rome became dominant with Charlemagne in the ninth century and earlier in Britain at the time of the Synod of Whitby in 664. Celtic Spirituality, which has undergone a revival in our own time with its Eastern Orthodox links and its sense of the sacred in nature and daily life and of the divine immanence and the intimacy of God celebrated in poems and hymns, was eclipsed. Its severity, desire for vengeance and excessive penance, tends to be overlooked by those who may be inclined to romanticize it.[1]

Bonaventure

Something of its emphasis was recovered in the thirteenth century by Thomas Aquinas, Francis of Assisi and, above all, Bonaventure (1217–74) who was in some sense to Franciscanism, what the Fourth Evangelist was to Christianity. It had represented a gentle devotion to the human Jesus and an awareness of his sufferings for us, in contrast to the Christ of doom, the strict judge consigning sinners to hell as depicted in many a sculpture or mural. The Christmas crib was an invention of St Francis. Bonaventure gave this a philosophy. He had been saved from death in infancy by the prayers of St Francis and it was natural that he should join the Franciscan order. His

interpretation of Francis, the Legenda Major, was, by a decree
of 1266, made to supersede all others. He used the three phases
of purgation, illumination and perfection to describe the spiritual journey. There was some feeling that he was in danger
of breaking the vow of poverty since he needed libraries provided by rich benefactors. Like John Henry Newman centuries
later, he did not divorce the intellectual and the spiritual life.
Nevertheless, the knowledge of God in his sweetness – a term
frequently used in medieval spirituality – is better and nobler
than intellectual research. The goal is union with God in love,
the crowning height an ecstasy which few attain. This has a
hiddenness and is beyond words. There is both illumination
and darkness. Bonaventure put this into words which Evelyn
Underhill said all students of theology should keep in mind:

> Ask grace not learning; desire not understanding; the sigh
> of prayer not industry in study; the Spouse not the master;
> God not man; mist not clarity . . . let us die, therefore, and
> by the door of death enter into this darkness. Let us impose
> silence on our anxieties, our concupiscences and upon the
> working of our imagination. Let us with Christ crucified
> pass from this world to the Father.[2]

Bonaventure's principal work was *Itinerarium Mentis ad
Deum* (The Journey of the Mind to God). The journey begins
with Francis' mystical experience and his receiving of the
stigmata, the wounds of Christ, at Averni. Bonaventure is
a Neo-Platonist with his belief that reality is spiritual and
intellectual, and demands the mental effort of philosophy. He
combines this with what Denys Turner describes as 'the almost
brutal concreteness and historical specificness of his meditations on the life of Christ in his *Lignum Vitae*'. He ends the
Itinerarium like this. It is necessary that we should

> die and enter into this darkness. Let us silence all our care,
> our desires and our imaginings. With Christ crucified let us
> *pass out of this world to the Father* (John 13.1) so that

when the Father is shown to us, we may say with Philip;
It is enough for us (John 14.8) ... For he who loves this
death can see God, for it is absolutely true that *Man shall
not see me and live* (Exodus 33.20).[3]

Bonaventure wrote to a poor Clare:

Draw near, dear handmaiden, with loving feet to Jesus
wounded, to Jesus crowned with thorns, to Jesus fastened
to the gibbet of the cross; and be not content as the blessed
apostle Thomas was, merely to see in his hand the print of
the nails or to thrust your hand into his side; but rather go
right in, through the opening in his side to the very heart
of Jesus where transformed by the burning love for Christ,
held by the nails of Divine love, pierced by the lance of
profound charity, and wounded by the sword of deep compassion, you will know no other wish or desire or hope of
consolation except to die with Christ upon the Cross, so
that you can say with St Paul: 'I am crucified with Christ
... I live; yet not I but Christ liveth in me.'[4]

Here is an instance of the long tradition of devotions to the
Passion. This has been both Catholic and Protestant, though
more visual in the former with sometimes frightening images
of the suffering Jesus, centred upon the crucifix. Although
such images did not enter Christian art for some centuries, they
have dominated it ever since. Isaac Watts' eighteenth-century
communion hymn 'When I survey the wondrous cross' has
been called 'a Protestant crucifix'. By the fourteenth and fifteenth centuries, as has been said, 'the Passion became the
chief concern of the Christian soul'. But it begins with
Anselm's *Cur Deus Homo?* explaining that Jesus, the perfect
man, makes satisfaction to God for the dishonour done by us
sinners to his majesty and sees him as such as our brother. He
takes pity on us 'his kindred and brethren' and pays our debt.
For Bonaventure as for Francis, the prayer of the Passion
was the supreme means of obtaining union with Christ by

love. In a book of meditations attributed to Bonaventure, in its translation by the Carthusian, Nicholas Love, 'probably the most popular vernacular book of the fifteenth century',[5] the events of the Passion are distributed according to the pattern of liturgical hours in the Primer. The meditative soul is to be present at the events of the Passion 'effectively, busily, thoughtfully and perseveringly'.[6]

Union with God-in-Christ was the goal of Bonaventure's journey. It led to an ecstasy which few could attain, but which is expressed in many evangelical hymns, notably Wesley's 'Thou shepherd of Israel and mine' based on Canticles (Song of Songs) 1.7, in which Calvary is that 'happiest place', 'where saints in an ecstasy gaze and hang on a crucified God'. And in the middle ages, a time of plague and death, the Passion of Christ showed a God who was not only far-off Judge but present in Jesus our brother, afflicted in our afflictions. This is typified by the altarpiece at Grünewald in which Christ is shown on the cross, his body racked not only by wood and iron, but by the plagues and poxes of human flesh, while at the foot his friends crouch in terror and a silent John the Baptist points – 'Behold the Lamb of God who takes away the sin of the world.'

Bonaventure begins Chapter IX of the *Legenda Major* with a polished and lyrical account of St Francis' response to the world around him:

Everything incited him to the love of God, he exulted in all the works of the Creator's hands, and by the beauty of his images, his spirit rose to their living origin and cause and by the traces impressed by God he admired Supreme Beauty in all beautiful things and by the traces impressed by God on all things, he followed the Beloved. To him all creation was a stairway which led up to him who is the goal of all desires. With an intensity of devotion unknown before him, he enjoyed the delights of the fount of joy in every single creature, as in rivulets flowing from it. He perceived celestial harmonies in the concord of the virtues and activities which God had given the creatures, and, like the prophet David, he was sweetly reminded by them to praise the Lord.[7]

This links Franciscan spirituality to the nature mystics and it is significant that the passage has been found copied out in one of Gerard Manley Hopkins' undergraduate notebooks. Francis and his followers knew 'the dearest freshness deep down things'. Francis might have appreciated the lines of George Meredith, which the headmaster of Tonbridge School inscribed in the resplendent copy of Thomas Browne's *Religio Medici* that he gave to the young Charles Raven on his departure to join the Second Division in France in April 1917:

> Into the breast that gives the rose
> Shall I with shuddering fall?

Francis died at his own request naked in the dust of Mother Earth and his great Canticle of the Sun which he composed during a time of total blindness, pain and immobility at the end of the winter after he had received the stigmata, does not select nosegays from a sheltered garden, but praises God for the fierce elements and for bodily death. He preached, as all the world knows, to his sisters the birds; he also called himself 'the little brother of the lice'.

The mystic or romantic poet sees more than the black letters of the book of nature. He looks with 'the inward eye' to that which is beyond sense perception or the test-tubes and computers of the physical sciences, 'the mystic heaven and earth within'. He is the opposite of the reductionist, who sees, not only through the window into the garden, but through the garden too and ends in nothingness. Francis saw Christ everywhere – in the lambs which reflected Christ's meekness and which he wanted to buy back from slaughter, in the rock on which one should walk warily lest one trampled underfoot the Son of God.

It was his participation in Christ which gave him kinship

with the whole creation. The Canticle of the Sun could not have been conceived apart from the stigmata. There are not two little poor men, the one so congenial to us in his joy in the world around him, simple, sane, exemplary, the other so morbid in his brooding on the tortures of the cross, driven blind by his tears, a manifest case of abnormal psychology. The key to his penetration through the world to God is that grace of poverty by which having nothing we yet possess all things. Thus his oneness with nature made him plead courteously with the fire which was to cauterize his face in a barbarous and vain attempt to cure his blindness and is all one with the love which, near the beginning of his way, made him overcome great revulsion of feeling to kiss the hand of a leper.

The mass

The high middle ages in particular saw the increasing dominance of the mass with many paraliturgies and legendary developments of the Christian story. For the devout it was the focus of their devotion. The host, however, was to be seen not consumed. The Mass was the supreme act of contemplation, and from 1200 the exposition of the host was the high moment when all should kneel in adoration. This does not deny participation, but merely changes it. The one who gazes becomes mystically incorporated in the miracle. Both the then Anglo-Catholic Bishop of Ripon, John Moorman, and a Quaker lady with whom I once had discussion, acknowledged that though communion was denied them by Roman Catholics they could in this way share fully in the benefits of Christ. Communion took place at Easter, which was a person's 'rights', though conditional, as the later Prayer Book has it, on being 'in love and charity with your neighbours'. Margery Kempe, who desired communion daily, was an exception to normal practice. Lady Margaret Beaufort received once a month, which was rare. It has often been said that the mass for most was an individual devotion as it is in Thomas à Kempis' *The Imitation of Christ*. Eamon Duffy has shown that this was far from the truth. If Sunday high mass was observed from a distance and the words of consecration said silently by the presiding priest that the people might not be hindered from praying their own prayers, or that the awesome words might not be accessible and profaned, there were daily masses at side altars to which people might draw near, and sometimes crowd around. Masses were parish occasions, furnished with vestments and lights by lay benefactions and obituary gifts and, as the middle ages wore on, at the centre of the constitution of guilds. And communion on one's death bed, the last sacrament, was no lone act. 'The hour of death was not one of isolation, but itself an experience of community.'[8]

Christ's Passion dominated the mass. Wounds and blood inspired devotion. The priest's vestments, so important to distinguish his unique and indispensable role and to separate him from the laity, came to represent the instruments of Christ's Passion, the maniple on the arm the rope by which Christ was led from 'tyrant to tyrant', the chasuble to recall the purple vestment in which Christ was mocked. Yet the prayers provided for worshippers, chiefly at the elevation, 'emphasized the glorious and risen nature of the body on which the devotee gazed'.[9]

There was an important transition in early medieval spirituality. The mass became less of a eucharist, an act of thanksgiving, more a sacrifice. This is a tendency found also in Gregory the Great (540–604). Kenneth Stevenson has shown that it is found in Isidore of Seville in the early seventh century and the Mozarabic rites.[10] It was to dominate Catholic understanding, but is also found in the Wesley Hymns on the Lord's Supper (1744) based on the Anglican Brevint.

The extent to which the mass penetrated the common life in the centuries before the Reformation has not been known since 75% of the population attended mass every day.

Death affected spirituality as it has done until our own time when, apart from accident and war, people live much longer and death does not seem to be around every corner. Purgatory was considered by Protestant Reformers to be one of the worst doctrines of Catholicism, implying a state of appalling physical torment, corrupted by the belief that it could be alleviated by good deeds done on earth and the sale of indulgences. It was 'old hell writ small', its only difference, admittedly vital, was that only the saved had to undergo it. The threat of purgatory was intended to spur the living to penitence and action. Freed from its extremes it helped to solve the problem that so few seem ready for the immediate beatitude of God's presence. In Dante, as later in Newman, whose *Dream of Gerontius* almost convinced the English scholar Basil Willey of its truth, 'rational and charitable though unscriptural', purgatory was of the divine mercy. It was a process of healing not of punishment. There was hope and grace amid the pain and certainty of salvation, though some were left in doubt.

Baron Friedrich von Hügel and others in our century have seen belief of purgatory as all of a piece with 'the inevitability of gradualness' in the way to holiness. The Wesleys seem to have believed that perfection could be immediate, as sudden as was sometimes first conversion. At death the hopes, aspirations and achievements, though still tainted by mortal limitations and incomplete, could by a miracle of grace be brought to full fruition. As an evening hymn has it:

> Or if thou my soul require,
> Ere I see the morning light,
> Grant me, Lord, my heart's desire,
> Perfect me in love tonight:
> Finish thy great work of love
> Cut it short in righteousness
> Fit me for the realms above.
> Change and let me die in peace.

For the evangelical Christian to be 'accepted in the beloved' was all that mattered. This overcame all lingering faults.

Belief in purgatory meant that the dead were not forgotten. It also strengthened kinship. Unshriven mothers could be brought to penitence and a state of grace through the intercessions of their children. The intercession could be corporate and formalized in offices and masses and the provision by the better-off of chantry chapels with their own priests.

Mysticism

There was a growth in mysticism. This is a complex term, which some think should be abandoned in favour of the earlier term 'contemplation', but it does stand for an immediacy of access to God and of union with him. It frees prayer from being tied to history – Christ is the first-born of many and with us here as truly as with his first disciples. It makes God accessible to everyone, but it could divorce faith from reason and while overcoming 'the scandal of particularity' remove the decisiveness of the incarnation and atonement done once and for all. It is not exclusively Christian as is demonstrated in William Johnston's book, *Mystical Theology: The Science of Love.*[11] In 1957 V. A. Demant said: 'There is a truly Christian mysticism such as we find, for example, in Ruysbroeck and Saint John of the Cross; there is a good deal of mysticism that is not Christian as in Plotinus and Eckhart and much good Christianity which is not mystical at all.'[12] Many would challenge the reservations over Meister Eckhart though there was controversy as to his orthodoxy in his lifetime and in 1329, the year after his death, twenty-seven of his propositions were condemned by Pope John XXII. The problem is partly that he was a preacher, and a proliferation of sermons, not always carefully written down and argued like a theological treatise, may lead to inconsistencies, contradictions and confusions. There is evidence that Eckhart did proclaim somewhat recklessly that he was in the Godhead before he was created, that there is that in the soul which is God, so that the highest part of the soul, the intellect, meets God in a conversation of erotic mutuality. It is 'a contact, meeting and union of what is esentially superior with the highest point of the inferior, in which both sides kiss each other and embrace in a natural and esential love that is inward and very delightful'.

Denys Turner has said that '*Some* version of the soul's

ultimate identity with God is the common stock in trade of the whole Western mystical tradition, at least until as late as the sixteenth century and he has also shown that there is a difference between the mysticism of the middle ages and that of the present.[13] Dom Cuthbert Butler put it more simply when he denied the use of the term mystical to 'occasional concomitants as visions, revelations, raptures or other psycho-physical phenomena'. The word should be kept for the sense 'given it in the beginning by "Dionysius" – the secret knowledge or perception of God in contemplation'.[14]

The mysticism of the middle ages is:

1. A union of Neo-Platonism and Scripture. This is found in Gregory of Nyssa, Cappadocian but of great influence in the West, and Dionysius or Denys the Areopagite, fictitiously the convert of Paul on Mars Hill, but in fact an unknown author of the sixth or seventh century, though understandably because of the quality of his thought, until the sixteenth century credited with near apostolic authority. Both Gregory and Denys interpreted the story of Moses' ascent of Sinai in the terms of Plato's allegory of the Cave where the one who escapes is dazzled by excess of light.

2. There is an alternation between the apophatic saying what God is not and the cataphatic rich and varied descriptions of the Divine mystery. The former rests on the assumption that in Aquinas' words, 'we do not know what kind of being God is', between us and him is what an anonymous writer would call 'the cloud of unknowing' which cannot be pierced by the intellect, only by 'the sharp dart of longing love'. Theological knowledge is in fact to 'unknow'. The *via negativa*, the negative way, is the way to God, beginning from what he is not rather than a supposed knowledge of what or who he is. As Meister Eckhart wrote:

> You should love God as he is non-God, a non-spirit, a non-person, a non-image, but as he is a pure, unmixed bright 'One' separated from all duality; and in that One we should eternally sink down, out of 'something' into 'nothing'.[15]

The cataphatic element is the opposite, to quote Turner, 'the verbose element in theology', a 'verbal riot' and this does not only consist in words, metaphors, technical terms, expositions, but in the non-verbal, liturgy and sacrament, music, architecture, dance and gesture.[16]

For Denys God is light but also darkness. And then he negates the negation by saying that God is 'a brilliant darkness'. There is a paradox in mystical language. We must name God. Denys found fifty-two names for God in Scripture. All are inadequate. They demand incompatible attributes. God, for instance, cannot be both male and female, though to name him in terms of the male gender alone does not do justice to experience, or even to Scripture. God transcends all language.
3. Detachment is necessary if there is to be an immediate knowledge of God. Our religion must no longer be man-centred but God-centred. We must abandon ourselves, even our desire for our satisfaction in God, the blessings and advantages faith in him might bring, even our religious 'experience'. And we shall not seek the removal of hindrances but accept them as the situation in which God calls us to respond. Demant quotes Dom John Chapman's *Spiritual Letters*:

> The essential interior act of religion is the giving ourselves to God, turning to him and remaining turned, uniting ourselves to his will and renewing this union as often as we think of it, or simply remaining united. When this essential act is going on in the point of the soul, all the rest of the soul can be in disturbance, unrest, rebellion, misery – it does not matter – on the contrary the 'point of the soul' accepts it, embraces it, wills it.[17]

For Eckhart, detachment is a more fundamental virtue than love. It is complete self-emptying. It leaves the soul open to God alone, all images and concepts of God are removed. It is complete poverty of spirit, not even the desire to do God's will. Eckhart comes near to the quietism which Wesley was to deplore in the Moravians. But in fact for Eckhart detachment means the abolition of distinctions between the interior life of devotion and outward practicalities of service. He will have none of the polarization of Martha and Mary. John Burnaby quotes Rudolph Otto: 'Martha with her never-wearied doing and acting proves that she has already found what she desires and seeks: the deep unmoved repose at the centre in unshakeable unity and security.'[18]

To be detached one must live without explanation, 'without a why'. We may compare Simone Weil's assertion that Christianity does not seek a supernatural explanation of suffering, but a supernatural use for it. Eckhart would not be happy with the term or concept of 'spirituality'. Earlier in the partial quotation above, Eckhart had said that the love of God must be stripped of all spirituality. He does not disparage the ordinary ways of devotion, but God himself is beyond all our images, analogies and conceptions. We must become detached from them lest we worship our own conception of God and not God himself, who is beyond all that we ask or think.

4. Compunction, piercing, is the preliminary to contemplation. Gregory the Great (540–604) has been called the 'Doctor of Compunction', though it is found in Benedict and in the harsh Irish ascetic Columbanus (c.543–615), not to be confused with Columba. He has a sermon 'On Compunction' which includes an impassioned prayer that Christ may set his heart aflame with love. Gregory distinguishes two kinds of compunction. The soul is first pierced with fear and later with love. There is first bitter weeping in sorrow for sin but then in confidence of pardon, the soul 'is inflamed with love for heavenly joys ... Thus the perfect compunction of fear draws the intellectual soul to the compunction of love'. Private reading of Scripture may pierce the soul with the dart of pain and the sword of compunction. The tears of penitence lead to tears of love. Compunction is total commitment to the whole Christian life. 'To hear the spirit's voice is to rise up in love to the invisible Creator by the power of intimate compunction.'[19]

5. There is in mystical experience a dark night, a period when

we are denied the consolations of religion, God seems absent
and all that is left is a round of duties. In the sixteenth century
John of the Cross discerned two dark nights. There is the night
of the senses, in which we have to renounce the earthly things
which separate us from God, and the night of the soul, an
agonizing stage in which we feel that God has taken himself
away and left us helpless.

The conventional teaching is that this is a sign that one is
called to union with the divine love but must be taught to love
God for himself alone and not for his benefits, for love to be
disinterested as in that Spanish sonnet of which a Latin version
has been made into a hymn attributed to St Francis Xavier.

> I am not mov'd, my God, to love of thee
> By heaven which thou dost pledge me as reward.
> I am not mov'd to cease to grieve thee, Lord,
> By thoughts and fears of hell which threaten me.
> *Thou* mov'st me, O my God. Mov'd sore am I
> To see thee nailed upon that cruel Tree,
> The scorn of men, wounded despitefully.
> Mov'd am I: thou dost suffer and dost die.
> Mov'd am I thus to love thee: yea
> Were there no heaven at all I'd love thee still;
> Were there no hell my dues of fear I'd pay.
> Thou needst not make me gifts to move my will,
> For, were my hopes of heaven quite fled away,
> Yet this same love my heart would ever fill.

There are problems. What is the relation of the dark night to
the 'cloud of unknowing', to the apophatic way? And is this
different from psychological depression or melancholia, a matter which concerned John of the Cross? Denys Turner has
investigated this at some length and concludes that the difference lies in that 'what the depressed person hopes for in her
depression is the restoration of the lost self-image and its
corresponding self-motivating power of agency, whereas the
passive nights "deconstruct" not only the identity we once

possessed but also that whole panoply of "possessiveness" from which derives the need to possess one at all'.[20]

6. Mysticism in a term used by William Johnston may be called 'the science of love'. The divine love is its goal. 'Intelligence cannot reach up to it because of its *transcending union of love*.' 'Rise up to union with God by means of the highest love.'[21] This love is brought about by the remembrance of Christ's passion as we have seen in Bonaventure. It is expressed in the rhyming jubilus 'Jesu the very thought is sweet' attributed to St Bernard of Clairvaux.

Dean Inge said of Bernard:

His great achievement was to recall devout and loving contemplation to the image of the crucified Christ, and to found that worship of the Saviour as 'the Bridegroom of the Soul' which in the next centuries inspired so much fervid devotion and lyrical Christian poetry.[22]

At the same time Bernard repudiates brooding on the physical details of the Passion. To know Jesus and him crucified is not to see him with no form nor comeliness in our weak flesh. It is to think of him as whole Christ, victorious in glory, though as a consequence of wounds and death.

Julian of Norwich in a vision of 1373, during an illness for which she had prayed looking on a crucifix which a priest held up before her, had a long and vivid vision of Christ's sufferings, the blood trickling down from his face. But David Knowles has pointed out that the pictorial element is small and subordinate and though 'vivid, indeed extremely so, is in a sense abstract rather than photographic': 'The "bodily sight" does little more than release a deeper shewing in the understanding, and this in turn leads, not at once but over a space of many years, to a purely spiritual and largely incommunicable sight or contemplation of the divine truth behind the true previous forms of manifestation.'[23]

Is this different from the ideas of Bonaventure considered

above? It has not dominated spirituality in which, as comments on 'Seeing Salvation' the millennium exhibition of pictures depicting Christ's sufferings showed, there is obsession with what Charles Wesley, to the discomfort of his brother John, called 'that dear, disfigured face'.

The chief source of Bernard's teaching is his eighty-six sermons on Canticles (The Song of Songs). He also teaches that one must advance from meditation, which he calls 'consideration', to contemplation. This is an ascent to calm repose from the simple tasks of piety and liturgy. 'The grace of contemplation is granted only in response to a long and importunate desire. And it is not given to everyone, but to those chosen to be the Bride of Christ. The opening words of Canticles 'Let him kiss me with the kisses of his mouth' represent three stages of the spiritual life – purgative, illuminative, unitive. We must first kiss Christ's feet in penitence and sorrow; and then his hand which will lift us up to fulfil the works of piety; and then we dare to kiss, united with him in one spirit.

Bernard is not afraid to use the erotic language of the Song of Songs, though emphatically resolved to distance himself from any suspicion that sexual love is hallowed by it. A man and woman are not to be thought of in this context, but rather the Word of God and a human soul, and more particularly, Christ and the church. It is as a member of the church that the individual is the Bride of Christ. Contemplation is both of the intellect and of the heart, one in discernment the other in fervour. The latter is a momentary foretaste of heaven. There is a distinction between pure contemplation, in which, says Dom John Chapman, 'reason as well as imagination remains in darkness and nothing is understood by it', and revelation in which 'the pure intellectual conceptions are made comprehensible by means of the imagery or words which the mind habitually employs'.

Contemplation is like the sleep of the soul in the arms of God, but it is no quietism. 'The soul itself is full of light and operating with intense activity.'[24] On the other hand it is as a sleep, a dream, not a face to face encounter in this life.

All mystical writers would stress the transience of contemplation in this life, the recoil of the soul afterwards. There is the alternation of God's presence and absence, but Bernard does not talk of the dark night of the soul.When the intense joy of contemplation is over, the spiritual marriage remains.
7. Dom Cuthbert Butler points out, perhaps a trifle disparagingly, 'that the line of great seers of visions and hearers of revelations is made up almost wholly of women'. He refers to Gertrude and the Mechtilds and goes on to list other well-known examples:

Hildegard, Elizabeth of Schonau, Bridget of Sweden, Angela of Foligno, Catherine of Siena, Maria Magdalena de Pazzi, and in modern times, Margaret Mary Alacoque and Catherine Emmerich. Until Butler's day, Francis of Assisi was the only case of stigmatization among men. He comments, 'There is something in the make-up of women that renders them susceptible to this kind of quasi-mystical experience'.[25]

Denys Turner notes that Eckhart's vernacular sermons were preached mainly to women, which may be one reason why he fell foul of inquisitors.[26]

What is important is the feminism of Julian of Norwich and, earlier, of Anselm of Canterbury. In his Prayer to St Paul there is this:

But you, too, good Jesus are you not also a mother? Is not he a mother who like a hen gathers his chicks beneath his wings? Truly, Lord, you are a mother too.

In the fifty-eighth and fifty-ninth chapters of the long text of her *Showings*, Julian says: 'As truly as God is our Father, so truly is God our Mother'. In the Trinity he is the power and goodness of fatherhood and the wisdom and lovingness of motherhood. It is the second person of the Trinity who is our Mother, our brother and our Saviour. From this it follows that as truly as God is our Father, so truly is God our Mother. 'Our Father wills, our Mother works, our good Lord the Holy Spirit confirms.'

And so Jesus is our true Mother in nature by our first creation and he is our true Mother in grace by his taking our created nature. All the lovely works and all the sweet loving offices of beloved motherhood, are appropriated to the second person for in him we have this godly will, whole and safe forever both in nature and in grace from his own goodness proper to him.

I understand three ways of contemplating motherhood in God. The first is the foundation of our nature's creation; the second is his taking of our nature, where the motherhood of grace begins; the third is the motherhood at work. And in that by the same grace, everything is penetrated, in length and in breadth, in height and in depth without end; and it is all one love.[27]

8. Is the contemplative life open to all? Augustine recognizes that hermits, for instance, have unique advantages, but Christ's 'little ones' who are not intellectuals, but follow the way of Christ crucified may attain it. Gregory the Great preached about its possibility in sermons. Bernard was preaching to monks and, as we have seen, denies that all are chosen to be contemplatives, but there are passages such as this:

'My beloved is mine and I am his'. It is the Church that speaks thus. But what shall we say of each of us individually? Are we to think that there is anyone among us to whom what is said by the Bride is capable of being applied? Anyone, do I say, among us? I should think that there is no one at all among the faithful members of the Church with respect to whom it may not justly be inquired whether the Bride's mystical saying is not in some degree realised in him.[28]

The fullness of contemplation may not be attained by all. It is confined to those who are Brides of Christ, members of the church and already united to him. Of these none is totally excluded.

Chapter 4

The Eastern Church

After centuries in which they shared a common Christianity with some differences and disputes, the Roman and Byzantine churches split in 1054 and have remained so. Attempts at reconciliation have so far failed and the end of the cold war has made the Orthodox Church less ecumenical, in spite of its membership of the World Council of Churches – membership which the radical theology of the 'third world' has threatened.

'The Eastern tradition' wrote Vladimir Lossky 'has never made a sharp distinction between mysticism and theology, between personal experience of the divine mysteries and the dogma affirmed by the Church'. Mysticism and theology support and complete each other.

One is impossible without the other. If the mystical experience is a personal working out of the content of the common faith, theology is an expression, for the profit of all, of that which can be experienced by everyone. Outside the truth kept by the whole Church personal experience would be deprived of all certainty, of all objectivity. It would be a mingling of truth and falsehood, of reality and illusion: 'mysticism' in the bad sense of the word. On the other hand, the teaching of the Church would have no hold on souls if it did not in some degree express an inner experience of truth, granted in different measure to each one of the faithful.

Lossky points out that the Eastern church has reserved the name 'theologian' for only three sacred writers, St John, most mystical of all the evangelists, whom the Orthodox Church believes is also the author of the Apocalypse, Gregory Nazianzen, writer of contemplative poetry, and St Symeon, known as the 'New Theologian', singer of union with God'.[1]

The liturgy is the life of the Orthodox Church. A very able and inspiring address I heard, entitled 'Orthodox Spirituality', was entirely about the liturgy. Metropolitan Anthony Bloom has criticized conventional Orthodox teachers for this and for neglecting prayer other than in the liturgy. In his own books, he has tried to remedy this.

There is a story of a young Englishman, member of the YMCA, who after a stay at Mount Athos, left in the company of one of the monks with whom he shared a journey of three days, staying in village inns. He was interested to observe what devotions the monk practised: apparently none. As they parted, curiosity overcame him and he asked for an explanation. The monk was surprised. To quote Patrick Hankey's account 'He pointed out that he was a member of a community – a worshipping body; every day and always the community offered its common prayer in liturgy and office. When he was there the monk took part in that prayer; and when he was not there he could not take part in it, but the prayer went on just the same. Was there anything else his young friend would like to know?'[2]

The Orthodox liturgy is not so much the recalling of Calvary, as in the Western mass, as the weekly journey into heaven, which one enters through the sacrifice of Christ. The kingdom is already realized beyond the altar. It is attained through the gift of Christ's body and blood made available through the Holy Spirit's descent upon the elements. A Catholic liturgist has said that 'the Orthodox Church has preserved the spirit of the early Church and continues to live by it and draw life from its source'.[3]

In spite of this the Orthodox Church has given much help in the understanding and practice of private prayer. It has done this by Hesychasm or the Prayer of Quiet, which is very ancient, probably derived from the desert fathers, though only committed to paper in the eleventh century in a treatise attributed to St Symeon the New Theologian. There was a belief that it went back to Mary, the Theotokos, Mother of the Lord, whom legend said had entered the Holy of Holies of the Jewish Temple at the age of three to learn contemplation.

It begins with entry into a state of quiet without ratiocination or books. There is repetition of the Jesus Prayer in one of its forms, such as, 'Lord Jesus Christ, Son of God, have mercy on me a sinner'. This is accompanied by control of the breathing. Symeon wrote:

Sit down alone and in silence. Lower your head, shut your eyes, breathe out gently and imagine yourself looking into your own heart. Carry your mind to your heart. As you breathe out say 'Lord Jesus Christ, have mercy on me'. Say it moving your lips gently or simply say it in your mind. Try to put all other thoughts aside. Be calm. Be patient and repeat the process very frequently.[4]

Some have recited the Jesus Prayer thousands of times a day. It has become their whole life.

Ecstasy is a phase at the very beginning of the process and should be temporary. Evagrius counsels that the one who prays must never try to see God in outward shape or form. All conceptions of God must go, so that 'the spirit becomes clothed with the ineffable beauty of the likeness of the Lord'. The power of love is not achieved by our prayer, but is communicated by the Holy Spirit. Unlike the thinking of Augustine, the Spirit is never thought of as the bond of love between the Father and the Son in the mystery of the Godhead. The Father is the sole hypostatic (substantial) source of the Holy Spirit, as in the original version of the Nicene Creed, in which the Spirit does not proceed from the Father *and* the Son but from the Father only. 'Love' used of the Holy Spirit does not describe his nature as the third person of the Trinity, but his nature as the giver of love, the source of love within us. This love is 'an uncreated gift, a divine and deifying energy in which we really participate in the nature of the Holy Trinity'. The words of II Peter 1.4 are fulfilled.[5]

There has been much controversy over Deification or theosis, rumbustiously dismissed by Ben Drewery in *Christian Spirituality*, and more gently by John Burnaby in *Christian Words and Christian Meanings*; found in seventeenth-century Anglicanism and in Charles Wesley by Donald Allchin in *Participation in God*.[6] In the Orthodox Church deification must always be understood in terms of Gregory Palamas' distinction between God's essence and his energies. The latter alone we may share. We do not become God in his being but we participate in his life and are transfigured by his love and radiance.

Eastern spirituality is not, as in some Western sources, the imitation of Christ, but of life in Christ. And the dark night of the soul is alien to it. St Bernard, of course, does not teach it in the West and an eighteenth-century Orthodox saint, Tikhon Zadonsky, did undergo it. But Lossky describes two distinct ways to sanctity since the separation between East and West. The latter 'proves its fidelity to Christ in the solitude and abandonment of the night of Gethsemane, the other gains certainty of union with God in the light of the Transfiguration'.[7]

The spirituality of the Eastern church is iconic rather than pictorial. The images with which the churches are clustered are not realistic representations, as in Leonardo da Vinci's 'Last Supper' in which one wants to know the identity of those around the table, but redolent of spiritual meaning and in the case of the Supper concentrated on the divine mystery of the eucharist.[8] The intellectual quest does not condition everything. Worship could never be described as 'a learning experience'. The way is apophatic; before one enters into union with God, one must, as we have seen, divest oneself of the intellectual and regard its categories as void. There is a danger here of a lack of humanity, a reluctance to question and also to change.

This is a corrective to the belief in the West which has had much recent currency, that change is the principal work of the Holy Spirit, but the Eastern view may leave the church corrupt, unreformed and inhospitable to new discoveries about nature and human nature.

Chapter 5

The Reformations

It is important to remember that there were two sixteenth-century reformations consequent on a revival of religion evident in the late middle ages. There was the Protestant Reformation to which the title is usually reserved, but in referring to the second reformation it is better to speak of the Catholic Reformation rather than the Counter-Reformation.

John Bossy, in editing in the mid-1960s Outram Evennett's Birkbeck lectures of 1951, chose as title *The Spirit of the Counter-Reformation*, but he points out in an introductory paragraph that Evennett was convinced that 'spiritual rebirth and enlightenment . . . are not achieved by ecumenical councils; they occur in solitude or by contact with individuals who themselves have been spiritually reborn and enlightened'. In his first lecture Evennett discusses alternative names but retains Counter-Reformation which he sees as drawing its power and influence from the Latin countries, 'from that whole vivid, forceful civilisation of the late sixteenth and early seventeenth centuries'.[1]

The two reformations have much in common. Their way was prepared by the 'modern devotion' which arose in the Netherlands and Northwest Germany, exemplified in Geert Groote and the Brethren of the Common Life which, as in *The Imitation of Christ*, attributed to Thomas à Kempis, empha-

sized the individual's relation to God. In the high middle ages
asceticism, to use Max Weber's word, became increasingly
'intramundane', this worldly, less dominated by monasticism
as the honours school of holiness. The world itself was
enlarged by explorations and discoveries with immense political and economic consequences, promoting missionary zeal,
which was part of the revival and not simply consequent on
new countries and people. Meditation became the prime
method of prayer as in the modern devotion. Ignatius Loyola,
founder of the Jesuits, was the supreme teacher with his *Spiritual Exercises whereby to conquer oneself and order one's life
without being influenced in one's decision by any inordinate
affection.* This is not a book of devotion for the individual but
a most flexible manual for the spiritual guide who 'gives' the
exercises to the one who performs them. They are divided into
four 'weeks' but these are stages not rigid seven-day periods.
The first week demands a rigorous examination of conscience.
The meditations are about sin and hell. The second week con-
sists of meditations on the kingdom of Christ and the events
of Christ's life from the Nativity to Palm Sunday. The third
week is dominated by the Passion, the fourth by the Risen
Lord. The Ascension and Pentecost are, strangely, missing.
After the fourth week there are 'rules for the discernment of
spirits' and *inter alia* directions for 'thinking with the Church'
to safeguard orthodoxy. Evennett has described the Exercises
as 'this finely adaptable spiritual mangle through which men
were passed to be brought out new'.[2]

The Spanish Carmelites

The Spanish Carmelites, Teresa of Avila (1515–82) and John
of the Cross (1542–91) were both reformers. John was retained
for the Carmelites, whom he was about to leave for the stricter
Carthusians, by Teresa who persuaded him to try and initiate
among male Carmelites what she was beginning among
women. She had already returned the women to being 'dis-
calced', that is returning to the tradition of going almost

barefoot rather than with their feet comfortably covered. They both, and John in particular, suffered for their reforming zeal. Teresa was a vivacious and attractive woman, highly sexed, though this must not be allowed to give a superficial explanation of her teaching. Had she not renounced all for the monastic life, she might have been very much a lady of worldly morals. She had the greater sense of humour and was quite capable of saying to John, in effect, 'come off it boy' when he was too intensely serious. They have both been subjects of many learned studies, notably in the last generation by Allison Peers and in the present by Rowan Williams and Colin Thompson. A summary of the background is given by Thompson in his essay on 'The Spanish Mystics' in Ralph Waller and Benedicta Ward, *An Introduction to Christian Spirituality* (1999). Thompson is a world authority on St John on whose mysticism we have already touched in Chapter 3, following Denys Turner. John was the greater theologian. Teresa had no formal theological training and her thinking can be muddled, yet it helps to elucidate John's analytic subtleties. But unlike John, for whom meditation was a stage on the way to union with God, she never abandons meditation on the sacred humanity of Christ. She would never be considered close to Buddhism, as John has been, though both von Hügel and Rowan Williams have seen resemblances to Luther in her spiritual struggles. Teresa had her struggles too. She was convinced that Mary and Martha must always go together, the active and the contemplative.

John is one of the greatest lyrical poets in the Spanish language. Like other mystics he unites poetry and prose in the attempt to communicate the experience. The best English translation of his work is by the poet Roy Campbell.[3] John's prose works are commentaries on his poems, not least one on the 'dark night' based possibly on his own remarkable escape at night from a cruel confinement. It recounts a night-time journey to union with the Beloved, possible only because it is night, and illustrative of his teaching on the dark night of the senses and the soul. Earlier he had written the *Spiritual Can-*

ticle, probably while he was in prison for being more reformist than the reformers. Like so much else influenced by Canticles on which Origen and Bernard had so notably commentated, it sees the consummation of the life of prayer as mystical marriage.[4]

Both John and Teresa eschewed the occult aspects of mysticism. Teresa was embarrassed by levitation. Colin Thompson says that both 'hold together the polar opposites of Christian doctrine and experience'. They combine awe before the transcendence of God with intimacy of communion with him. They are individuals who believe life in community – possibly a small community where love of neighbour may be practised – essential to Christianity. And they believe in the authority of the church rightly understood. Teresa, in spite of inquisitorial suspicions, thanked God that she was with all her unique personal immediacy with God a daughter of the church. They contended for the primacy of love in society and condemned its evils. 'The journey of any individual soul takes place within the redemptive work of the Trinity, while the whole of creation is the palace in which the Son will engage humanity to himself and take it as his Bride'.[5] But the Christian life demands everything, whatever the cost in persecutions or in inward suffering.

Francis de Sales (1567–1622), Bishop of Geneva, was in Henri Brémond's phrase a 'devout humanist after some years of living with the terrors of Augustine's doctrine of predestination'. Kneeling before the statue of the black Virgin in Paris, he heard a celestial voice overriding the Eternal Decrees: 'I do not call myself the damning One, my name is Jesus.' After some years as a missioner to the Catholics of Chablais on the southern shores of Lake Geneva he became associated with those who wished to renew the religious life of France after the Reformation and in the 'brave new world' of exploration and discovery. In the difficult see of Calvinist Geneva, he wrote his two devotional classics, *Introduction to a Devout Life* (1608) and *Treatise on the Love of God* (1616). He founded a new religious order for women, the Visitation, in which he was chiefly associated with the widow Jane Frances Fremyot de Chantal in what seems to have been a model of friendship between a man and woman both of whom were unmarried.

Like the Ignatian Exercises, though gentler and less dominated by the thought of the terrible warfare against demonic powers, his writings assert that holiness is possible to those whose lives are entirely in the world. Devotion is like walking through a garden plucking nosegays, hardly Ignatian; it demands a good deal in 'remote preparation', good reading, holy thoughts and refined meditation. The *Treatise*, which he spoke of to Madame de Chantal as 'our book', says that the heart of love is mutuality, a union of eros and agape, our desire and God's free grace. God needs our poverty. The unity of God and man in Christ is not only the remedy for sin. It is the purpose of creation; in the words of Duns Scotus: 'All things are created for prayer'. Yet prayer is no easy escape from living, but the life of Christ, his perfect communion with the Father. Its price is the cross. 'Mount Calvary is the academy of love.'[6]

Protestant spirituality

Protestant spirituality has been well described by Alister McGrath in *Roots that Refresh*.[7] It is above all 'grounded and nourished in the study of Scripture'. It is to know God and be changed by God, but God in Christ. Christology is central. So is the priesthood of all believers. The knowledge of God is not the special preserve of the clergy nor is the testimony to Christ's saving power. And, as we have seen, for the whole of this period, holiness is concerned with life in the world.

For Martin Luther the central doctrine, the focal point, was salvation by faith alone. This was of great comfort to guilty sinners for thereby the righteousness of Christ was imputed to them so that they might grow into it, rather as an actor takes on the character of his part by putting on his clothes. It cannot be too strongly emphasized that Luther was a most devout and disciplined monk. As Gordon Rupp has said 'he drove himself nearly daft ... trying to follow the mystic counsels of

St Bonaventura until his common sense bade him desist'. He struggled with the matter of his election until his confessor von Staupitz told him to leave such thoughts and begin with the wounds of Jesus.[8]

For John Calvin the focus was union with God through Christ. The Christian life starts in the divine initiative, in God's gift in Jesus Christ as our sanctification, our prophet, our priest and king. Our whole salvation begins with God's grace and ends with his glory, but as Calvin's eucharist has it, we are made 'very members incorporate in the mystical body of his Son'.

The union is a great mystery. It is no mutual relation of separates. The New Testament speaks of it in terms of utmost intimacy, vine and branches, bread and eater. We are united to the glorified Christ in heaven by the Holy Spirit. 'Though it seems an incredible thing that the flesh of Christ, while at such distance from us in respect of space should be food to us let us remember how far the secret virtue of the Holy Spirit far surpasses all our conceptions and how foolish it is to wish to measure its immensity by our feeble capacity. Therefore what our mind does not comprehend let faith conceive, that the Spirit truly unites things though separated by space.'[9] Calvin grows lyrical about faith. It is complementary to the love of God in the mystical/contemplative Catholic tradition. It enables us to penetrate the heavens, it brings the very life of Christ into our souls, it means that we, while still on earth, may live the life of heaven.

The two Gospel sacraments make this union effective in the life of the church. To deny baptism to infants is to make the new covenant narrower than the old, in which there was circumcision on the eighth day. It must always be done visibly in the congregation.

Anabaptism or second baptism was endemic in the middle ages. Not only did it insist on baptism by faith but had a notion of brotherhood in which all barriers would disappear and peace and love prevail. It did not obtain the consent of the mainstream reformers because as John Bossy has said 'it dawned upon them that all kinds of things by which they set great store – the Christian instruction of children, the integrity of the Christian household, the identity of the church and the civil community – hung upon the traditional practice of infant baptism'.[10]

To return to Calvin, for him the Lord's Supper demands 'eschatological distance'. The Holy Spirit lifts us up to be with Christ. Christ does not descend to transubstantiate the bread and wine. The Supper constitutes the church. But word and sacrament must never be sundered, for it is the word which gives the sacrament its power, makes it more than dumb show and creates the fellowship of the faithful.

We must not dissociate ourselves from membership of the church, above all attend to its preaching and observe its discipline, even though not all members of the visible church belong to the invisible. There could be cruelty in the treatment of transgressors, as in Victorian novels whose characters are publicly denounced and cast out, particularly for sexual sins. Calvin was not a rigorist and felt the early church was too harsh in banishing sinners from holy communion for years and sometimes for life.

Prayer is the principal exercise and expression of faith. Thanksgiving is vital. Prayer is best in the words of Scripture; books may almost be a trifling with God. Prayer is wrestling and pleading. It is a sign of our union with Christ and must be offered in his name. When it comes to prayer for those who may not be of the elect, compassion always gets the better of logic. We may pray, says the Puritan William Gouge, in the words of the English litany 'that it may please thee to have mercy upon all men' even though the majority may not be of the elect.

Calvinist spiritual writers have not been blind to the wonders, joys and beauties of creation, they have not stifled the arts of music and poetry in particular, and they have sustained family life and family prayer and not only in bourgeois homes, as Burns' 'The Cottar's Saturday Night' makes clear. Calvinists would find it hard to see sanctity in Graham Greene's whisky priest or in Geoffrey Beaumont accom-

panying the Gospel with gin, 'in industrial quantities', and
cigarettes. It may have been too hard on permissiveness, but
must not be blamed for Scottish Sabbatarianism, New England
witch hunts, western capitalism, or South African apartheid.[11]

In a fine chapter in *The Poetry of Meditation*, Louis L. Martz
maintains that it was Richard Baxter in *The Saints' Everlasting
Rest* (1650) who taught Puritans to meditate in ways which
they would have regarded as pertaining to Catholic salvation
by works. This may ignore some of Baxter's predecessors.[12]
John Owen was opposed to mental prayer 'as pretended unto
by some in the Church of Rome'. It may disregard the
mediatorship of Christ and attempt to by-pass the parousia.
But he does not condemn 'holy meditations', which may be
enjoyed in mental or vocal prayer indifferently. 'The *spiritual
intense fixation of the mind* by contemplation on God in Christ'
is to be aimed at in prayer and results in the soul being lost
in admiration and delight. But this is the gift of Divine grace
not the achievement of devotional techniques leading to
irrational ecstasy.

Baxter teaches a sacramental meditation upon nature. We
must learn to open out the creation as well as the Bible and
'the several passages of providence and read of God and of
glory there. Certainly by a skilful industrious improvement we
might have a fuller taste of Christ and heaven in every bit of
bread that we eat and every draught of beer that we drink than
most men have in the use of the Sacrament.'[13]

Baxter's *Saints' Rest* was written out of bodily weakness and
illness as a comparatively young man and teaches meditation
chiefly on heaven. It is marvellously eloquent compared with
Ignatius Loyola's more utilitarian exercises for a director. Long
out of use, it could still inspire if read aloud.

Baxter believes that sense should be used as well as faith.
We should enter heaven in our imagination, picture its glories
and tread its streets. We should spend some time there every
day. This should be accompanied by Soliloquy 'a preaching
to oneself', and then from speaking to ourselves we speak to
God.

John Stachniewski, in his very important study, *The Persecutory Imagination*,[14] has shown that Calvinism could lead to despair, that there was a dark side to Puritanism at which I have hinted above. We see it in John Bunyan's struggles in *Grace Abounding*, but before that in Richard Norwood's autobiography, 1639/40, unpublished in its time. One of Stachniewski's book's strengths is its awareness of the social setting of English Calvinism: 'a heavily patriarchal culture in a vicissitudinous social world'. The pilgrimage of Christian in the first part of the *Pilgrim's Progress* is the exorcism of the despair which Calvinism created. Part II represents the more secure position of Dissent in society, which by implication it credits to the steadfastness of those like Bunyan who would not compromise nor treat with their opponents. Ignorance is the problem character whose fate spoils the ending of Part I. Stachniewski maintains that his fate is due to the fact that he ignores 'the persecutory imagination': he simply deceives himself into thinking that he has the experience of salvation; he has no validating certificate and if he can be admitted to the Celestial City, then all Christian's sufferings are in vain.

Stachniewski has to admit some softening in the Baxterian tradition. There are gradations of certainty and certainty differs with the evidences. The *Saints' Rest* may have been written to counter despair, but it succeeds in showing how the Christian may be led from 'an unfruitful sadness to a joyful life'.

Anglicanism

Anglicanism, if the use of the term in the seventeenth century is not an anachronism, is not, as Hugh Trevor-Roper has shown, a purely English phenomenon. It was dominated until the reign of Charles I by moderate Calvinism. 'It attracted French Huguenots like Casaubon, Dutch Arminians like Grotius, dissident Italian Catholics like Paolo Sarpi and Marcantonio de Dominis, Greek patriarchs like Cyril Lucaris.'[15] Charles I, under the influence of William Laud, made the church 'Arminian', a term which Laud did not like. It means, among other things, believers in free will and universal grace. Laud was a reactionary in church order and discipline, a persecutor of those who would not accept his liturgical impositions. For him, in contrast to Calvinism's focus on the pulpit, 'the altar was the greatest place of God's residence on earth'. (George Herbert (1593–1633) placed pulpit and prayer desk of equal height as ambos.) But in many ways Laud was a liberal in theology in that he sought freedom from dogma whether Catholic or Calvinist. He was charged with being a Socinian, i.e., one who gave supremacy to reason, or also, a follower of the Unitarian Faustus Socinus, a term which he much resented. On the scaffold he called himself a Protestant, though at that time the word 'protestant' included the designation of the word 'catholic'.

In 1637 he refused to license a reissue of Foxe's *Acts and Monuments* which had been placed in every parish church and was regarded by most Anglicans as next only to the Bible. It was prominent in the Ferrar community at Little Gidding. In his last sermon, Laud omitted to include Cranmer among those archbishops he most admired.

Trevor-Roper has brilliantly unravelled the intricacies in his essay on 'Laudianism and Political Power'. Laud's nominees at Puritan Cambridge built college chapels, John Cosin in Peterhouse with colours, candles and a strict discipline in attendance and behaviour. Cosin had produced his book of devotions based on the monastic offices to counter the Catholicism of Henrietta Maria's courtiers. It should be compared with Lewis Bayly, Bishop of Bangor's, *The Practice of Piety*. The *Book of Common Prayer* is common to both, but Cosin supplements it with monastic offices, Bayly with models of extempore prayers, long and theological, verbose in comparison. But these last have a Catholic source in the Spanish humanist, Ludovicus Vives (1492–1540) who came to England in 1523 as tutor to Princess (later Queen) Mary. The simple tasks and occasions of daily life must be associated with the events of the gospel and the great ends of providence. The bed is always to remind the sleeper of his grave, his rising of the resurrection. Should he hear the cockcrow he must remember Peter's denial and penitence with many tears. The putting on of clothes is to carry the mind back to man's primeval innocence and fallen shame. The sun streaming through the windows is to be a sign of the sun of righteousness risen with healing in his wings.[16] As an exile during the commonwealth Cosin became more hostile to Rome and was not so extreme in the liturgical discussions after the Restoration, but still contended for a revised Prayer Book. By contrast Richard Baxter and his liturgy, in its attempt to accommodate Puritanism, was in fact more catholic in its doctrine of sacrifice than the revised *Book of Common Prayer*, though it was never used. Laudianism, defeated during the Commonwealth, triumphed at the Restoration due to the so-called Clarendon Code and indeed has left its traces in the English church to this day. What did survive was Anglican liberalism represented by the circle brought together under Lord Falkland at Great Tew in Oxfordshire, in the 1630s, and which did not disappear with his early death in the Civil War. It has been treated both by Richard Ollard in *Clarendon and His Friends* (1987) and by Hugh Trevor-Roper in his essay 'The Great Tew Circle' (1987).[17] It was an intellectual movement. Its faith in reason meant that, like its mentors, Erasmus and Grotius, it did not regard scepticism as sin but as part of the rational process. 'It shall well befit our Christian modesty' wrote John Hales 'to participate somewhat of the sceptick'. Scepticism did drive some to suicide or near it and some to Rome. Chillingworth poped for a brief period until he found that Rome, though attractive and comprehensive from outside, was tyrannical within. His *The Religion of Protestants* was the great book of the circle, much influenced by Richard Hooker, the Elizabethan divine of the 1590s and the quintessential Anglican. Chillingworth found moral certainty rather than infallibility of one sort or another, established by reason. Like the others at Great Tew, where he had come to his settled position through much reading and conversation particularly with Falkland, he was conservative in that he wished change to be brought about by continuity not revolution and detested above all else violence and war.

He felt that the Church of England was nearest to the true church largely because 'of its non-theological character, its simplicity, its rationality, its historical claim to preserve the essential, ecumenical Christian philosophy'.[18] Clarendon, a member on whom Great Tew had perennial influence and its first historian, was no mystic. He dismissed contemplative prayer as tending to 'a dull and lazy lethargy'; 'a mortified and moping spirit incapable of any "magnanimous activity".'

The Great Tew circle were loyal to the King yet were opposed to Laudianism in its right wing aspects, its clericalism and its lack of ecumenism in that it disallowed the authenticity of continental Protestantism.

In all this we must not neglect the place in Anglicanism of the *Book of Common Prayer*. It had won, amid all opposition, by the magnificence of its language which lingered so wonderfully on the ear and the fact that use of it was proscribed and made illegal under the commonwealth so that it stood as a symbol of precious loyalties. Non-mystical, its ideal that of a 'godly, righteous and sober life', it was realistic for those who lived in the world, who knew well how tainted they were by compromise and sin, who had to live in constant penitence and yet dared to believe that it is by grace that we are saved. Unequivocally protestant, there could be unearthed a buried catholicism in offices, litany and eucharist and infant baptism. It became ploughed into the English soul, its phrases recalled more than those of the Authorized Version of the Bible. For four hundred years it bore the burden of a people's prayers.

Other sects and dissidents

There was a gallimaufry of sects and dissidents during the sixteenth and seventeenth centuries, not least in reaction against the establishment in the interests of a living faith and on behalf of the poor. Luther called Thomas Muntzer (1491–1525) an arch-devil. He was a revolutionary, anti-clerical and violent, and was rehabilitated by Eastern European communism. He had a deep devotion derived in part from the German mystical tradition and the modern devotion. As a liturgist he may be compared with Thomas Cranmer, some of whose work he anticipated, notably the reduction of the offices to two and the introduction of a vernacular Mass. Later he became something of an enthusiast believing in direct inspiration and placing great faith in visions and dreams. What began and continued in mysticism ended in politics, the politics of revolution.[19]

In England at the time of the Civil Wars and afterwards there were innumerable sects with which I have dealt briefly in my *John Bunyan the Christian*.[20] There were Puritans who passed into radicalism, which inevitably, was divided. There were Levellers, 'Arminians of the left' opposed at once to Calvinism and the church, compassionate, devoted to the Passion, but ready to fight oppression and defend the poor with force of arms. There were Diggers under the leadership of Gerard Winstanley, who believed that every one had a right to dig everywhere and believed that clergy and the universities were the enemies of truth and justice. Winstanley became a Quaker. The Ranters were mystical antinomians, anti-legalistic, indulging in sexual promiscuity and charismatic. The Fifth Monarchists, inspired by Daniel 7, believed that the reign of King Jesus would be based on Mosaic laws and had a clear political programme. Above all, there were the Quakers, destined to survive. Their founder, George Fox, may have been the greatest religious figure of the seventeenth century. In origin they were ecstatic enthusiasts, no serene and peaceful Society of Friends. Their meetings could be manifestations of shaking and trembling, hence their name. They were perfectionists who believed that Christ lived in them. He, the Holy Spirit, the inner light, had more authority than Scripture, which might be a dead letter. They were miracle workers continuing the works described in the longer ending of St Mark's Gospel. They hated the clergy and the gentry and subscribed to the myth that privilege, class and oppression dated from the Norman Conquest. They deplored sacraments as being empty ceremonies incapable of making the revolutionary change of heart they implied. They stressed the peaceful nature of the movement, though their pacificism after the Restoration was forced upon them by the outside world. They gave greater prominence to women than most religious bodies. Their tradition of silence may have originated in the need not to say anything which would give cause for gossip against them. They were bitterly persecuted, not least under the Commonwealth, though Cromwell had sympathy towards Fox. Later their purpose in keeping silence was not to attain the beatific vision so much as to find words to speak to each other.

Chapter 6

From the Eighteenth Century to the Present[1]

The English spiritual teachers of the early eighteenth century drew on vast resources old and new, but there was an impoverishing ignorance of and contempt for the Middle Ages

> Anglican rigorists like William Law knew little of the 'discretion' of St Benedict or the joy in creation of St Francis, while the great Bernardine tradition with its fine German inheritance through Hildegard of Bingen and the sisters of Helfta to say nothing of the great Victorines, was little known. There is in fact something faintly off-centre, exotic, about the mystic devotees at the beginning of the eighteenth century. They over-valued women like Antoinette de Bourignon and Mme Guyon, and saintly eccentrics like Gregory Lopez and M. de Renty counted for more with them than St John of the Cross or St Theresa.[2]

This was also true in France. In 1699 Rome condemned François Fénelon's *Explication des Maximes des Saintes sur la Vie Interieure* after the bitter and unedifying quarrel with Jacques Bossuet, but Fénelon's personality and teaching had a 'drawing loveliness' and his influence continued in the eighteenth century long after his death in 1715. Alexander Knox, the Irish Anglican *en rapport* with Wesley, declared that 'no Catholic was more popular in Protestant countries than Fenelon'. To love without thought of reward, to love even if one's final destiny is hell, is what every lover feels at times in the ardour of devotion and desire. It is the lover's hyperbole, but it is unchristianly individualistic, an *egoism à deux* – I must wish for others' happiness and the coming of the kingdom of God – and it denies hope.

Jean Pierre de Caussade (1675–1751) claimed that his teaching on contemplative prayer was not contrary to that of Bossuet or tainted with Quietism, which may roughly be defined as a passive waiting on God which dispenses with the outward and corporate professions of the Christian religion and even with philanthropy. The great watchwords of de Caussade's teaching are 'abandonment to Divine Providence' and 'the Sacrament of the Present Moment'. The former, though different from the Quietists' passivity, in some sense rehabilitates Fénelon in that 'abandon' includes being ready to accept the worst possible outcome in the knowledge that we are never out of the hands of God who is Love. The latter has proved of great value in our own time when the danger for so many is to wallow in the failures of the past, or constantly to be living life in the future in hope or dread of things to come.

The early eighteenth century in England saw the triumph of the moralists. The age of reason, the Englightenment, as it came to be called in 1860s Germany, replaced the passionate devotion with its acrimonious and sometimes bloody divisions of the preceding century. The eucharistic spirituality of a Lancelot Andrewes with its patristic inheritance and witty wordplay and the Puritan scholasticism of election, justification by faith and imputed righteousness were alike supplanted by the teachings of those who their detractors called Latitudinarians represented by an influential treatise, *The Practice of Christian Graces*, better known by its subtitle, *The Whole Duty of Man* (1658). This was written by a Royalist High-Churchman, Richard Allestree, but its ideal is that of the Prayer Book's 'godly, righteous and sober life'. Holy Communion is one of the Christian's duties, the fulfilment of which leads to holiness which is happiness. There is no teaching of contemplative prayer, which the Latitudinarians might have dismissed with Clarendon and John Owen.

The Non-Jurors continued the tradition of Caroline spirituality often in the form of a more extreme sacramental devotion, though Orthodox not Tridentine (i.e. pertaining to the Council of Trent). But their most famous representative, William Law, not wholly typical and much engaged in their irate infighting, always characteristic of separatist minorities, has a rigorist strain born out of a deep pessimism about human nature and a revulsion from human life, especially sex. In his denunciation of the stage, his rules about dress and cosmetics, his proscription of the profession of attorney, and his distrust of marriage, he is the typical Puritan of caricature, much more than those who, historically, bear that name. Yet his great treatises on *Christian Perfection* and *A Serious Call to a Devout and Holy Life* were of decisive influence on John Wesley, Samuel Johnson and, in the next century, John Keble. In later life, he was captivated by Jacob Boehme (1575–1624) the German mystic with his weird creation mythology and pseudo-Dionysian Hellenism, interspersed with moving affirmations of the Divine Love. He became reconciled to the Quakers whom he had earlier opposed, in his condemnation of oath-taking and war; and he wrote of the catholic spirit in words similar to those of John Wesley, not in terms of Church order and sacramental validity, but as 'a Communion of Saints in love of God and all Goodness' far transcending orthodoxy.

Joseph Butler, the greatest of the moralists, cannot be charged with 'enthusiasm' or extravagance. He was a sombre realist, aware that from many aspects this is a poor ruin of a world and that religion comes to us with apparent contradictions, its work half-done, its revelation incomplete. Yet he preached on the love of God in terms which have been called Augustinian.[3] His influence extended into the next century to Newman and Gladstone who in 1873 wrote that without him he did not think he ever would have been right. Butler speaks eloquently of our true happiness being in the love of God which is not a matter of self-interest. God himself 'may be to us all that we want', our life, our joy, our comfort and our portion for ever. His preaching soars at this point and is not without enthusiasm. He anticipates 'all that was deepest and truest in the Methodist appeal to the heart'.[4]

Butler, Law, the French and German Pietists, with their indebtedness to the English Puritans and their belief in prayer as the great instrument of love against sin, would be united in the Johannine assertion 'we love him because he first loved us'. But we must notice a tradition of 'affectionate' spirituality represented in the dissenting heirs of Richard Baxter, who combined theological eclecticism with deep seriousness and that catholic spirit Law and Wesley expounded.[5]

The leading divines were Isaac Watts (1674–1748) and Philip Doddridge (1702–51). They averred that there was a place for rapture and emotion in the Christian life, and that preaching might well be with tears, both with wonder at the divine love and sorrow for sins. Yet they knew the dangers of the rhetoric of affection. Watts wrote on Logic and *The Improvement of the Mind*. With a Miltonic confidence in reason, he combined the rational and the evangelical. His *Guide to Prayer* is chiefly concerned with public prayer. It offers a rigorous and full analysis of the parts of prayer. There are wise counsels on the use and abuse of book prayers and on posture. Doddridge, who delighted in prayer and lived often with God, and remained serene and confident amid many sorrows, was engaged in the training of ministers and preachers. He was on good terms with Anglicans and a protagonist of missions overseas. *On the Rise and Progress of Religion in the Soul* was written at Watts' instigation, has been translated into nine languages including Tamil and Syriac, and is a classic of evangelical spirituality, much used in the Church of England until our own time. It traces the development of the Christian life from first conversion to the honouring of God in death. He honours the ordinances, particularly the Lord's Supper, but he writes of the 'absence' of Christ in the sacrament, for 'he is not here, he is risen' and the Supper is not the heavenly feast. Yet it is a table spread with bounties as his much-loved hymn 'My God, and is thy table spread?' declares.

Hymns were a characteristic of affectionate spirituality and of Pietism as they had been of reformed and sectarian Christianity since the Reformation. But now they are an expression of rapture in Doddridge, in Watts, much the greater hymnographer, and above all with Charles Wesley. The last wrote hymns on the great Christian doctrines and on the experience and growth in grace of the individual believer, a conspectus of spirituality from conviction of sin, pardon, through the vicissitudes of the Christian life, to the attainment of perfect love. In this tradition hymns are both part of liturgy – they interpret and paraphrase Scripture and assist the movement of worship to its climax in eucharist and offering, whether or not the bread and the wine are there – and a means of grace in private devotion. They lift up heart and voice in song, sometimes expressing pathos and penitence as well as praise. They are also to be prayed in private. This has been the experience of Nonconformists and Methodists, of Pietists and Lutherans, of converted criminals on the way to the gallows, soldiers on the battlefield, Dietrich Bonhoeffer in prison, and many a believer, scholar or not, at the beginning and end of the day.[6]

Methodist spirituality

Methodist spirituality was a path to perfection. Like the Eastern Orthodox and the Pietists, John Wesley took seriously II Peter 1.4 with its promise that we may be partakers of the divine nature and 'the future imperative' of Matthew 5.48, that we shall be perfect as our Father in heaven is perfect. This implied the continual working of God's grace and the refusal to set any limits to it and it meant realizing the two great commandments, total love of God and neighbour. This perfection might be obtained even in this life, mortal and ignorant as we remain, through the 'means of grace'. Wesley divided these into the instituted means – prayer, private, family, public; Scripture, read, meditated, heard; the Lord's Supper, fasting and Christian conference – and the prudential means. These last included Wesley's own adaptation of the Groups or Societies which had been a feature of later seventeenth-century spirituality both in England and France, and which were found among the Moravians. The Methodist Bands, Societies and Classes, into which converts were divided, were intended both for fellowship and mutual spiritual direction. The revolutionary aspect of this is not only that it is 'societary' ('help us to help each others Lord') but that it is lay. The 'directors' are not officials duly set aside, but ordinary men and women with a knowledge of God.

Wesley's spirituality was, in the words of George Croft Cell, a synthesis of the Protestant ethic of grace with the Catholic ethic of holiness. It has been said that the Wesleyan revival was not only evangelical, but sacramental, and this is true in that Wesley believed that the Lord's Supper was not only a 'confirming' but a 'converting' ordinance and that Methodist celebrations, more frequent than was usual in the parish churches, were thronged with enthusiastic receivers. The *Hymns on the Lord's Supper* (1744) was a best-seller. It is largely a paraphrase of the Anglican Daniel Brevint's *The Christian Sacrament and Sacrifice* (1673) with an affirmation both of the real presence and the eucharistic sacrifice which seemed to some Anglo-Catholics of the next century to be a harbinger of the Oxford Movement. But it is doubtful whether the high doctrines registered with the majority of Wesley's converts, though the belief in the sacrament as of perpetual obligation did.[7]

The Evangelical Revival

The Methodist Revival was only part of the eighteenth-century Evangelical Revival, which was largely Calvinist in theology as against Wesley's Arminianism. Selina Countess of Huntingdon (1707–91) was one of the few of the nobility who experienced evangelical conversion, as Ronald Knox once wrote, 'not so much a conversion from sin, as a conversion from righteousness'.[8] She used her wealth in philanthropy, but also to propagate Christianity, particularly among her peers, in contrast to Wesley's penchant for the lower middle classes and the poor. She attracted the great evangelical preacher George Whitefield and many able young clergymen, but she eventually quarrelled with Wesley since she feared his Arminianism made him flirt dangerously with salvation by works. In the early 1780s she had to separate from the Church of England, and form her own 'Connexion', with its own ordained ministers, owing to court action against her building a Chapel in Spa Fields, London, which resulted in all her proprietary chapels being regarded as homes of Dissenting congregations. Newman paid her tribute in the next century. He was much moved 'by the sight of a person simply and unconditionally giving up this world for the next . . . She acted as one ought to act who considered this life a pilgrimage not a home'.[9]

The Church of England Evangelicals also preferred not to desert the parochial system for Wesley's itinerancy. Their work was done from settled pulpits, and although not all of the nobility, like Selina, they were often drawn from the wealthier classes. It is not insignificant that one of their greatest preachers and pastors, Charles Simeon (1759–1836), converted through reading *The Whole Duty of Man*, was Vicar of Holy Trinity Cambridge from 1783 until his death. Their appeal was to those who would become leaders of society, like those interrelated families who were to form the Clapham Sect in the early nineteenth century.

Their spirituality was based on preaching to convert, instruct and guide. Hearing the Word was all-important, but attendance on public proclamation was accompanied by a regular life of early rising, prayer in private and in household, the daily portion of Scripture studied and interpreted conservatively, and Sabbath observance. The Christian week from Sunday to Saturday was more important than the Christian year. The Olney hymns of John Newton, the converted slave captain, and William Cowper, 'the stricken deer' as he called himself, the poet often plunged into melancholia, were their staple diet. Prayer meetings were looked on by John Newton 'as the most profitable exercises in which a Christian can engage'. They had nothing of that reserve which was so characteristic of the Tractarians. They were much engaged in social work, for instance William Wilberforce and the emancipation of the slaves and, later, Lord Shaftesbury (1801–85) and the Factory Acts. Missions overseas were no less a priority than with the Methodists.

Later in the nineteenth century they became more revivalist. The Keswick Convention (1875) led to a holiness movement. Hymns with choruses became popular not least as a result of the Mission of the American evangelists Moody and Sankey in 1882. Sentimentality crept in as throughout Victorian life (though also doubt and agnosticism).[10] We think of the novels of Charles Dickens, though the fervent expression of emotion is not wholly to be deplored, as when the hymn 'Safe in the arms of Jesus' was played at Lord Shaftesbury's funeral in 1885 by the band of the Costermongers' Temperance Association. Choruses have remained a part of evangelical spirituality and have proliferated in the last quarter of the twentieth century often with mantra-like repetitions. They are usually traditional in language and imagery without the theological profundity of Watts, Wesley or Cowper.

There has been profound evangelical teaching on prayer as in Ole Hallesby's book of that title which has been in print for more than fifty years. 'Helplessness united with faith produces prayer', he writes, 'without faith there can be no prayer'. Even so, for prayer to become our element, the miracle wrought by the Holy Spirit is necessary (cf. Rom. 8.26). Yet there is a link with the contemplative tradition: 'Prayer is something deeper than words'. 'To pray is nothing more than to lie in the sunshine of God's grace.'[11]

Roman Catholic spirituality and its influence

Roman Catholic spirituality continued the sixteenth-century strain of 'holy worldliness'. Richard Challoner's *The Garden of the Soul* (1740) is indebted to Francis de Sales. After a doctrinal summary it provides devotions for each part of the day. Alban Butler's *The Lives of the Saints* published between 1756 and 1759 is a sober study presenting the saints as examples of life in the world. The mass and Mary were central to Roman Catholic devotion. The tabernacle on the altar was the focus of much prayer both in private visits and in extra-liturgical services such as Benediction. Piety was individualistic. One prayed at the mass rather than praying the mass. There was much rather tawdry baroque art and much meditation on the physical sufferings of Christ in his Passion as in F. W. Faber's hymn, 'O come and mourn with me awhile'. Faber is at times over-sentimental, addressing Mary as 'Mamma' for instance yet movingly proclaiming the infinity of the love of God.

John Henry Newman, convert from Anglicanism, brought his own spiritual genius to the Roman Church. His too was a spirituality of 'the trivial round, the common task', in the words of his Anglican friend John Keble's poem. Keble reminded him of St Philip Neri whose Oratorian disciple Newman became. Newman's counsels were often humdrum, 'go to bed in good time and you will be perfect'. His was a unitive spirituality of the whole person, body and soul. You do not only feel the movement of the heart towards God; 'you go to church, pass along the aisle to the holy table, receive Christ's body'. And it was unitive of clerical and lay, there was no holiness of the one different from the other; and unitive of all Christian people, 'promoting mutual sympathy between estranged communions and alienated hearts'.

Baron von Hügel (1852–1925), the Austrian nobleman who lived in London and wrote in at times tortuous and teutonic English, was much influenced by Newman, though he thought him too depressing ever to be canonized. Von Hügel distinguished three elements in religion, the mystical-emotional, the historical-institutional, and the intellectual-scientific. Each was necessary. He himself was a friend of the Catholic modernists, but survived their condemnation and was a typical Catholic in his devotions which included visits to the Blessed Sacrament.

He wrote an epoch-making book on *The Mystical Element of Religion* (1908) and was himself a renowned spiritual guide, turning Evelyn Underhill from God-centred towards Christo-centric religion. His counsels are enshrined in *Letters to a Niece* (1928) and other writings include the wisdom of his own confessor the Abbé Huvelin.

The Oxford Movement, which dates from 1833, sought to recover the catholicity of the English church against its being an arm of the state and a pawn of politicians. In its beginnings it was concerned with spirituality rather than ceremonial. Its leaders saw in the *Book of Common Prayer* buried catholicism which it was their mission to revive. They reacted against Methodism and evangelicalism, which sought salvation by emotion and excitement and cheapened the divine mystery. Reverence was the first disposition of the Christian mind. E. B. Pusey was their 'doctor mysticus' and there is contemplative rapture and ecstasy as he unfolds the mystery of union with Christ, above all in the eucharist. Benedicta Ward has recognized 'the huge silence and great quiet' of Nitria, Scetis, and the Cells within Pusey's nineteenth-century pages.[12] Yet he translated French Roman Catholic works on Confession.

The movement broke free of Oxford and found its mission in the slums, where it borrowed the splendour and colour of the Roman Church and illegally used the Missal and much else. It restored the religious life. It was at its best when it was a Caroline revival rather than a Tridentine importation. In the mid-twentieth century, it produced what has been considered its own 'school', represented by Bede Frost's *The Art of Mental Prayer* (1931) and especially F. P. Harton's *The Elements of the Spiritual Life* (1932), a rigorous and thorough account of Christian asceticism in Roman categories. Martin Thornton, in several books, distinguished an English School of Spirituality based *inter alia* on 'the speculative-affective synthesis', the liturgy, habitual recollection and spiritual direction. But he ignores Protestantism except in its more modern, radical guise and the Prayer Book tradition. A fine exponent of Anglican Catholic spirituality for the twentieth century is

Michael Ramsey, notably in *Sacred and Secular* (1965) and *Be Still and Know* (1981).

Spirituality of the late twentieth century

Later twentieth-century spirituality has produced a vast armoury of books of all kinds. Ecumenism has resulted in a free flowing of the spiritual life and traditions. Ignatian spirituality has transformed practices of prayer across the denominations, not least among Baptists. Spirituality has run parallel with radicalism sometimes as a refuge from its icy blasts along the journey, sometimes as its natural partner. The medieval Meister Eckhart, rightly or wrongly, is seen to teach a holism which frees the adherents of historic religions from 'the scandal of particularity' and the confinement of creeds and finds echoes in those aware both of our kinship with nature and the burning need of social justice. Don Cupitt denies the objective truth of God yet spirituality is central to the Christian life, but it must be autonomous. It cannot depend on external circumstances not even on God. Mysticism, which earlier in the century was given new vogue by Inge, von Hügel and Evelyn Underhill, is in the ascendent. The English mystics have greater circulation than in their own time and, as we have seen, there are many fine studies of the Carmelites, Teresa and John of the Cross. Mysticism appeals because of suspicions of history, which is uncertain, at the mercy of changing interpretations and new discoveries, and, dirtiest of words 'élitist'. It also rests on personal experience.

The descendants of those who opposed mysticism as often delusory and leading away from ethical activity, Kierkegaard, Oman, Reinhold Niebuhr and not least Bishop Charles Gore, seem silent, possibly for the reason given by Owen Chadwick. We are aware of the impotence of words. We carry on our dialectic in the dark; before God we are blind. Yet there is an overwhelming conviction of the purpose and the reality of (his) light.[13]

There may be discerned a drift away from the Jesus of

history spirituality of the decades to 1970, in spite of the techniques of Ignatian meditation. The liberal school of the first fifty years taught a meditation which, in the words of John Ruskin, sought 'to be present as if in the body at each recorded event in the life of the Redeemer'. There is now less certainty about the records, the confession by some of a vast ignorance about many of the details of Christ's earthly life. Do we touch more than the outskirts of his ways? Other faiths which cannot be dismissed as heathen errors, and whose spiritualities, Buddhism, Yoga, Transcendental Meditation for instance, influence many Christians, challenge his finality. Yet he is still seen, though through a glass darkly, as the window into God and the cry of dereliction is felt to be the word of God for the age of Auschwitz. At the same time there are new spiritualities of power world-wide, even what some would call Christo-Fascism. Liberation theology among the poor and oppressed, particularly in Latin America, is fearful of the pessimism and morbidity of a Christian emphasis on the tragic. And the Charismatic Movement with its speaking with tongues, has brought freedom and confidence and deliverance from inhibitions for very many. Black spirituality is now experienced in the West and North and has a fervour and convinced faith and a power of extempore prayer which some feel shames the agnosticism of the sophisticated half-believers. In some places the longer ending of St Mark's Gospel seems to be fulfilled.

The eucharist has retained and increased its hold with new liturgies and a more communal understanding, though less sense of mystery and adoration. Communion at 8 a.m. followed by non-communicating high mass at 11 a.m. at which one pondered and adored, and which turned the young Michael Ramsey from Congregationalist to Anglo-Catholic, has now almost disappeared. But many would agree with John Burnaby that there is in 'the memorial of the precious death and passion of God's dear Son, a safeguard against misunderstanding or misuse of the act of prayer which no defects in verbal expression can remove'.[14] Intercession with all its problems is for many the part of prayer which seems most real to them and the eucharist its supreme place, even to the extent of some moves to restore it to the canon itself.

Feminism is bound to have effect on spirituality which cannot as yet wholly be measured. How far will it go? The prominence now given to women spiritual guides of the past, the value of women as teachers and directors, the use of inclusive language, are now established at least officially. But what of our understanding of God and of truth and error? Will this be revolutionized with old 'heresies' rehabilitated and new images of God with spiritualities of creation and the womb?

Creation spirituality not only recalls Eckhart and others of the past, but would substitute 'original bliss' for 'original sin'. Dualism is the primary error. Compassion is the goal, which means justice and celebration, 'Extrovert meditation' is its spiritual technique. It offers four ways: creation; letting go and letting be; birthing; new creation. It has much in common with liberation theology and feminism. It recalls us to reverence for the earth. Its belief in the spiritual efficacy of art such as we see in the writings of Don Cupitt, may ignore the deep unhappiness and wrecked lives of many artists, their melancholia and suicides, though note the discussion of Hans Urs von Balthasar below.

The New Age movement has some affinities with Creation spirituality. It is complex and syncretistic with an emphasis on global issues and millenarianism. Christians are bound to be cautious, yet must not simply be hostile and fail to recognize its challenge.

There has been some decline in the monastic life, but there has been creation of communities, mixed and including the married. Iona, founded by George Macleod, was the pioneer but Taizé, originally intended to unite Protestants and Catholics, where the brothers are celibate, has a far-extending influence. And both – and others – are agents of spirituality, reviving worship and prayer allied to manual work.

Not the least hopeful sign results from the work of Roman Catholic theologians, such as Karl Rahner and Hans Urs von

Balthasar influenced by the work of Karl Barth. Balthasar has written a Theological Aesthetics and there is much interest far and wide in the spirituality of beauty and art including retreats arranged for the study and practice of painting. But above all these theologians are Trinitarian, seeing the kenosis or divine self-emptying (Phil. 2.7) as no temporary and temporal event, but the eternal action and passion of the triune God. They teach contemplation the apophatic way, but this concerns the Transcendent One who reveals himself in the divine action of the incarnation and the cross and calls us to that union which is a sharing in his sacrifice for the whole world.[15]

There is also Donald Nicholl, who died in 1997, more honoured in Anglicanism than Rome. An academic at Keele and Tantur, his outstanding book, first published in 1981 is on 'holiness'. I have summarized it at the end of my book on *Methodist Spirituality*.[16] It is written from Nicholl's experience of human life in many continents. It insists that holiness is for all, not for the specially gifted and mystically inclined and draws examples from many faiths, though the supreme instance is of the Christ of the Incarnation and Calvary. The Passion, the one final sacrifice for the whole creation, is inescapable. Holiness involves our whole selves, body and soul. It also demands self-sacrifice and suffering.

The Methodist J. Neville Ward, in many works, most notably *The Use of Praying* and his study of the Rosary, *Five for Sorrow, Ten for Joy*, interpreted Catholic spirituality for today with the eucharist as the focus of prayer from which our daily prayers flow.

An immensely influential teacher is Thomas Merton who died in mysterious circumstances in Bangkok 1968, but whose writings still command world-wide readership and re-publication. Born in 1915, he had a dissolute youth, wasted his time at Cambridge. He got a young woman with child, but abandoned her and went to America. He entered Columbia University, became devoted to literature with a particular interest in William Blake and Gerard Manley Hopkins as well as Dante and was converted to Roman Catholicism. He was also devoted to jazz. In 1941 he joined the Order of Cistercians of the Strict Observance or Trappists and remained for twenty-seven years in the monastery of Our Lady of Gethsemane in Kentucky. The paradox is that as a Trappist he wrote not only poetry but autobiography and works on contemplative prayer. He thought Julian of Norwich and John Henry Newman the two greatest English theologians. He was concerned with politics and at the end of his life was opposed to the Vietnam war. He never lost interest in Buddhism and it was his desire for liaison between Christianity and Buddhism which took him at the last to Bangkok.

He was, it has been said, a theologian of the cloister not of the lecture hall and he belongs to that great tradition which sees the theologian as the person of prayer and makes no distinction between the intellectual quest and the mystical life. He much loved the writings of Hans Urs von Balthasar. Monasticism was a way of life which was possible outside the cloister. It demanded detachment from the ordinary concerns of the secular world, preoccupation with the inner ground of one's religious and philosophical beliefs, and a special concern with inner transformation and a consciousness of the transcendent beyond the self and pious practices. Contemplation cannot of itself change the world, but without it 'without the intimate, silent, secret pursuit of truth through love, our action loses itself in the world and becomes dangerous'.

Dietrich Bonhoeffer, the Lutheran pastor, killed by the Nazis at the very end of the second war for complicity in the Hitler bomb plot, has had immense influence through his three books, *The Cost of Discipleship*, *Ethics* and *Letters and Papers from Prison*. He felt that the Christianity of the future would be 'religionless' and secular. He was aware that through modern discoveries God had handed over many of his prerogatives to humanity. He agreed with Karl Barth that 'religion is not salvation'. In Spain he was much attracted to the mystics, but back in Germany he felt that the Bible was the effective weapon against the Nazis.

He saw it as a secular book, critical of much religion. 'The world must not be prematurely written off ... Christ takes hold of a man in the centre of his life.' God is not a *deus ex machina*. 'The Bible directs (man) to the powerlessness and suffering of God; only a suffering God can help'. Prayer is to kneel with Christ in Gethsemane and with him to cry out forsaken on the cross. 'The God who is with us is the God who forsakes us'.[17]

Secular Christianity had its vogue and still lingers, as indicated in the 'Churches Together in Britain and Ireland' report of 1999, which suggests that we may be nearer to Christ in the supermarket than saying 'pious prayers in Church'. Prayer was still necessary for secular Christians, though not always at fixed times and as a sterile duty. Petition with its tyranny of 'request–response' was a low level in spite of the teaching of Jesus. Iris Murdoch wrote: 'Prayer is properly not petition but simply an attention to God which is a form of love.'[18] Contemplation was not only the highest form of prayer but for some it might be the beginning as Michael Ramsey said in his F. D. Maurice lectures.[19] Or, in the existentialist language of Ronald Gregor Smith, not altogether alien to the eschatology of the New Testament, 'Prayer is to be understood as the anticipation in the whole of our existence of that one end which is the reality of God ... It is the engagement of the whole life in the hope of the End in Christ'. This has affinities with eschatology, of the Lord's Prayer 'Thy kingdom come'. I remember a sermon of my youth in which the minister mentioned someone who enjoyed the hymn 'Thy kingdom come' 'because it always goes with a rip'. 'Dare we say that', he declared, 'of the prayer which broke Christ's heart?' Gregor Smith would agree. This petition took Jesus not to the easy success of the poised and integrated personality but to the desolation of the cross. It did not summon legions of angels to his deliverance but left him in utter reliance on the power of the Spirit alone. 'The Spirit is the only power in the world. But the Spirit is power in powerlessness.'[20] And so, with Bonhoeffer, 'only a suffering God can help'.[21]

This would discard an attempt through religious exercises

to fix the mind on God. The recall of friendships, of the best moments of the past, 'a chorus ending from Euripides', a Mozart sonata, a game of cricket, or the torrent of Niagara might be what the philosopher, Bishop of Durham, Ian Ramsey called 'disclosure situations', while one lived amid the vicissitudes and sufferings of humanity by the stark realism of faith.

The continuing search

It is sometimes said that the religious alternatives today are Evangelicalism of a conservative nature or Roman Catholicism, with a rather outmoded liberalism representing a minority in between. The last of these does not, however, ignore spirituality.

Peter Baelz who died in March 2000 was one of the outstanding liberal scholars of our time. He called himself in Lacordaire's words 'a penitent Catholic but an impenitent liberal'. He was successively Dean of Jesus College Cambridge, Regius Professor of Moral and Pastoral Theology at Oxford and Dean of Durham. He gave the Hulsean lectures on 'Prayer and Providence' in 1966. In them he attempts to relate the vigorous anthropomorphism of Scripture to an acceptable philosophy which takes due account of the world as we know it. The book is a closely-packed theological and philosophical study which demands close reading and response. No more important work on prayer has appeared in the past half-century, but it does not seem to have had a dominant influence. It is a reasoned reinterpretation of the Christian tradition, which, while it ignores no difficulty, is as acutely critical of the critics as of Christianity itself. It nowhere disregards or despises religious experience, and it does not, like so many discussions both traditionalist and secular, loftily assume that the prayer of asking, which is conversation with a personal God, is philosophically intolerable and religiously naïve. 'The ascription of personality to God is an attempt to hold together the religious and moral sides of human life in a unity, since it is in interpersonal relations that we discern the possibility of a harmony of giving and receiving, of acceptance and activity.'[22] Prayer teaches us how to participate in the mind and activity of God. Recognizing what God has already done, it will always have the note of thanksgiving. Looking forward to what God has still to do through those who respond to his love, it will also have the note of petition and intercession. Petitionary prayer is the confluence of divine providence with human faith. It is both a resting in God and a wrestling with God. There is protest, but on the other side is communion with God and dependence on his will.[23] 'We may give the love of God a *point d'appui* so that through our prayer it may realize the possibilities that only this way it can actualize.'[24] That God suffers must be admitted. This is no imperfection, though it is a limitation. It is rather the consequence of the fact that God is ever receptive and is temporal, not as we are for whom time means change and decay, but in the sense that while his love is perfect, his joy increases and is enriched by the response of his creatures. There is much that is in sympathy with John Burnaby's Hulsean lectures on love in St Augustine. 'Love never forces and therefore there can be no certainty that it will overcome. But there may and there must be unconquerable hope.'[25]

Some would dismiss Maurice Wiles, Regius Professor Emeritus of Divinity at Oxford, as a spiritual teacher with his work on the remaking of Christian doctrine and his argument that Christianity is possible without incarnation. His latest book *Reason to Believe*[26] is both a clear account of traditional faith and a summons to continuing search in the light of ever-developing knowledge, for neither Christian insights nor modern discoveries can lay claim to certain knowledge. But Wiles has also written a recent essay on 'Belief, Openness and Religious Commitment' which shows that openness of mind and examination of new truth is not incompatible with Christian dedication and in *Faith and the Mystery of God* he makes the same plea for continued search free of over-confidence. Faith requires 'the readiness continually to test, to review and where necessary to revise both the traditional affirmations of faith and its contemporary insights. And when I try to do that I still find myself convinced of a personal reality at the source of things – one whose character of love is most fully evoked by the figure of Jesus in that parabolic way in which alone the ultimate can be articulated and whose presence is most fully evoked through life shared with others in the Christian community.'[27]

In *Reason to Believe*, Wiles says that the purpose of worship is 'to shift our attention away from ourselves and concentrate it on God as the ultimate embodiment of goodness and love'. Petition and intercession raise difficulties when we can no longer believe so categorically in the providential ordering of the world by an interventionist God. But they are forceful ways of ensuring that our rightful concerns and the needs of others, sometimes desperate, are not forgotten or ignored in the context of worship. 'God is not the magician who adjusts the particularities of life at our request, but God is one whose loving presence has the power to transform our experience of every eventuality of life.'[28]

What is most interesting is that at a time when some, encouraged by Roman Catholic theologians such as Hans Küng, are saying that the doctrine of justification by faith is obsolete, Wiles, the once evangelical, argues that allowing for shifts of meaning, 'the phrase can properly assert that basic attitude towards God that underlies the kind of saintliness I am seeking to describe and that seems to me characteristically Christian'.

It implies that our fundamental standing in the world is determined by the acceptance of God's free and gracious love for us and not by our own merits or our own achievements. And it provides not only the answer to the sins of the mighty, the tendency to pride, arrogance and superiority; it provides also the answer to the needs of the weak. In a very fine passage Wiles argues that justification frees us from the fear that the tragic element in life which is everywhere and inescapable does not destroy ultimate value and meaning. 'That is secure, secure by virtue of the graciousness of God.' We are justified by faith. Jesus himself is 'the prototype of the justified person'. He knew no sin but he lived by faith to the end.[29]

Conclusion

'The Groundwork of Christian Spirituality' is what modern jargon calls 'the Christ event', that is Jesus in history and subsequent experience, in Martin Kähler's words 'the historic Christ in his fulfilment'. The debate about the Jesus of history and his relation to the Christ of faith continues. Sometimes one feels that to found faith on Jesus of whom much is unknown, uncertain and disputed, does not give intellectual or theological security. But he has haunted the human mind since his death and is the paradigm of the Christian's relation to God though interpreted in many ways, as recently by Dominic Crossan in *The Historical Jesus* and by Geza Vermes in *The Changing Faces of Jesus*.[1]

There is now as never before in our interconnected world the question of other faiths and other founders. What of Buddha and Muhammad, to say nothing of Moses? Their differences from one another and from Jesus must not be forgotten in the lazy belief that in their life and teaching they are essentially the same. This is far from the case. And we must not idealize them. The faults apparent and so rightly deplored in Christian history are not absent from the history of other religions. It is not only the Pope who needs to say 'mea culpa'.

I am inclined to maintain that Christianity is unique in its doctrine of the Incarnation, which may have influenced other religions rather than being part of their own inheritance. I have found R. C. Zaehner's inaugural lecture 'Foolishness to the Greeks' convincing on that score.[2] But there must be respect for other faiths and a desire to discover their truth and enhance our Christian spirituality by learning from them, as well as a missionary willingness to share our Christian experience with them.

Christian spirituality today will be ecumenical between the various forms of Christianity in that there will be a willingness to learn and understand denominations other than our own. The unitive spirituality of John Henry Newman is essential, 'mutual sympathy between estranged communions and alienated hearts'. We shall not unthinkingly condemn dissidents from the orthodoxy we may hold, and dismiss protest when it assails our convictions. I have already mentioned Thomas Müntzer (p. 89 above). Much earlier, there were the Montanists in the second and third centuries, ecstatic, enthusiastic, claiming the spirit of prophecy and living by an austere, unworldly discipline. There have always been those who have reacted against establishments, fearful of Christianity's alignment with 'the powers that be', the worldliness and prosperity of the church, 'caesaro-papalism' and the loss of what A. N. Whitehead called 'the Galilean vision of humility'.

I have hardly mentioned one whom, in my 1969 book, *The Life of the Spirit in the World of Today*, I called the 'prince of protestors' – Søren Kierkegaard. His *Attack Upon 'Christendom'* is devastating in its assault on formal, socially acceptable Christianity, baptism as a pretty ceremony with godparents who have no idea how to keep their promises, attendance at the Lord's Supper an interlude between getting and spending, marriage half-erotic, half-Christian. How different from the awesome sacrifice of Christ and the total transformation of life he demands! Kierkegaard writes outrageously and his own experience was somewhat warped. Yet he stabs us to the heart.[3]

Spirituality today unites contemplation and action as with St Teresa and Thomas Merton. There must be what Iris Murdoch called 'loving attention'. Evangelicals would still believe in an interventionist God who arranges our lives for us if we will give heed. There are many testimonies in, for example, the BBC Songs of Praise programmes, to God's action in human lives. Others find this difficult.[4] Dorothy Emmet cannot imagine a Divine consciousness to which simultaneously 'all hearts are open, all desires known and from whom no secrets are hid'. Catholic teaching insists that at the Day of Judgment every individual will be aware of every sinful act done in the whole of his or her life, along with all the consequences, and God will presumably be aware of this for each and every individual. 'Even with the assistance of the Recording Angel', Emmet writes 'I cannot imagine any personal mind able to think of all this detail at once, and if it is said God can do so, I would say that one who thought like this would be a monster. I would hope that the penitential state before God could be thought of as the Kierkegaardian call to 'Purify your hearts', the chastening experience of knowing oneself as one is, or what the Psalmist calls 'truth in the inward parts'.[5] Emmet finds the orthodoxy of the creeds now impossible but not the gospel teaching of Christ's self-sacrifice as the heart of the universe. She has written of 'efficacious grace', a deep creative power 'which instead of feeding a ruthless will to live can feed a will to love, purifying the self-centredness of the will'. She believes in this rather than in divine causation of outward events.[6]

Iris Murdoch says that with attention 'goes the idea of grace, of a supernatural assistance to human endeavour which over-comes empirical limitations of personality. What is this atten-tion like, and can those who are not religious believers still conceive of profiting by such an activity?' She suggests that 'God was (or is) a *single perfect transcendent non-representable and necessarily real object of attention*; and I shall go on to suggest that moral philosophy should attempt to retain a central concept which has all those characteristics'.[7]

Against these reservations may be advanced the arguments of Peter Baelz in his *Prayer and Providence* – see p. 107 above. And there is an almost unanimous belief that in Bon-hoeffer's words 'only a suffering God can help'.

So much spirituality of the past depended on belief in a life beyond this and this life as a pilgrimage towards the perfect life of God after death. There is much less affirmation of immortality these days compared with W. R. Matthews' broad-cast talks of the mid-1930s or John Baillie's *And the Life Everlasting*. This is partly due to the awareness that human beings are a psycho-somatic unity and it is difficult to conceive of 'soul' apart from the body. But if one believes in God as revealed by Jesus and the possibility of a living, personal relationship with him in this life, it is hard to think, in spite of death's seeming finality, that it ends the communion. To believe that this life is a rehearsal of dying and a preparation for some fuller life beyond, though we know little of its details and it is shrouded in mystery, should not deter us from service of the world. It should enhance our belief of the crucial impor-tance of this life. The way we live here affects our eternal destiny.

Finally. Spirituality must be concerned with society and not simply with inward religion. This is exemplified in a fine symposium edited by L. Gregory Jones and James J. Buckley *Spirituality and Social Embodiment*. It forms a wonderfully comprehensive study relating spirituality to the world we are in, from Bernard of Clairvaux to African American spirituality today. It attacks the consumer approach to spirituality. There is new light on the New Testament, Aquinas, Julian of Norwich and Luther. It underlines much of what I have tried to contend but in profound depth of detail. 'To be a theologian is to pray truly and to pray truly is to be a theologian.'[8] And spirituality must have political and social implications. It is not only to pray but to vote.

If I were to suggest a book which encapsulates a spirituality for our time, I would be tempted to turn to the posthumously published spiritual diary of Dag Hammarskjöld Secretary-General of the United Nations, killed in the course of duty in 1961. Somewhat controversially translated by Leif Sjberg and W. H. Auden and introduced by the latter, it was given the title *Markings* and although a best-seller was found rather bewildering until Dr Henry P. van Dusen attempted a corre-lation with the outward events of the great civil servant's career.[9] The work is a twentieth-century example of the old

Puritan advice to keep a diary. It shows that each outward event of Hammarskjöld's life was anticipated by an inward conflict, each battle was fought and won within himself even before ever he was engaged in public affairs. It shows how, after many struggles within himself, he was helped to return to the beliefs of his upbringing through the ethics of Albert Schweitzer, who also provided him with a modern key to the world of the gospels.

> But the explanation of how man should live a life of active social service in full harmony with himself as a member of the community of the spirit, I found in the writings of those great medieval mystics for whom 'self-surrender' had been the way to self-realization, and who in 'singleness of mind' and 'inwardness' had found strength to say yes to every demand which the needs of their neighbours made them face, and to say yes also to every fate life had in store for them when they followed the call of duty as they understood it.[10]

As he progressed he became more biblical, more sensitive to the Christian year and more conscious of the living God of Pascal and Buber. He was often in the *Book of Common Prayer* and its Psalms. Eckhart had great influence. One of his famous sayings is that 'in our era the road to holiness necessarily passes through action'.

Notes

What is Spirituality?

1. V. A. Demant, *A Two-Way Religion*, Mowbray 1957, p. 14.
2. II Timothy 1.7.
3. Maxim Gorky, *My Childhood*, Penguin 1961, passim.
4. I John 4.1.
5. Lawrence Stone, *The Past and the Present*, Routledge and Kegan Paul, 1981, p. 19.
6. Ronald Knox, *Enthusiasm*, Oxford University Press 1950; R. Newton Flew, *The Idea of Perfection in Christian Theology*, Oxford University Press, 1934.
7. John 17.15.

1. The New Testament

1. Robert Carroll, *When Prophecy Failed*, SCM Press 1979.
2. Rowan Williams (ed.), *The Making of Orthodoxy*, Cambridge University Press 1989.
3. E. Hoskyns and N. Davey, *The Fourth Gospel*, Faber and Faber 1947, p. 460; cf. John Ashton, *Understanding the Fourth Gospel*, Clarendon paperback 1993, p. 465.
4. Luke 11.1.
5. Luke 11.9 cf. Matthew 7.7, 21.22; Mark 11.24.
6. G. M. Soares-Prabhu, *Concilium* 1990, p. 33.
7. J. Austin Baker, unpublished paper.
8. Luke 11.13; Matthew 7.11.
9. James Barr, 'Abba Father', *Theology*, May 1988, pp. 173ff.
10. Rudolf Otto, *Kingdom of God and Son of Man*, 1938, p. 20.
11. Matthew 11.25–6 and Luke 10.21.
12. Mark 8.34, Luke 9.23, and 14.25–27.

13. J. C. O'Neill, 'The Origins of Monasticism' in Rowan Williams (ed.), *The Making of Orthodoxy*, Cambridge University Press 1989, pp. 270ff.
14. Stephen Barton, *The Spirituality of the Gospels*, SPCK 1992.
15. Luke 5.27–32; Matt. 9.9–13; Mark 2.13–17.

2. The Spirituality of the Early Church

1. A. F. J. Klijn (ed.), *The Acts of Thomas*, Leiden 1962, section 144, pp. 142–3, quoted by Robert Murray 'The Features of the Earliest Christian Asceticism', in Peter Brooks (ed.), *Christian Spirituality*, SCM Press 1975, pp. 70f.
2. Luke 24.44 cf. verse 27.
3. Genesis 14.18; Psalm 110.4; Hebrews 7.
4. Joshua 5.13ff.
5. Daniel 3.24ff.
6. Psalm 137.9.
7. Henri Crouzel, *Origen*, T&T Clark 1989, p. 71.
8. Andrew Louth, *Origins of the Christian Mystical Tradition*, Oxford University Press 1981, p. 64.
9. G. F. Nuttall, *The Puritan Spirit*, Epworth Press 1965.
10. Kenneth Kirk, *The Fourth River*, Skeffington and Sons, London, 1935.
11. Andrew Louth, *Discerning the Mystery*, Oxford University Press pp. 106ff.
12. Andrew Louth, ibid., pp. 101ff., 130ff.
13. Gordon S. Wakefield, *The Liturgy of St John*, Epworth Press 1985, p. viii.
14. A. L. Lilley, *Prayer in Christian Theology*, SCM Press 1924, pp. 21f.
15. Clement, Stromateis 7.40.
16. Rowan Greer (ed.), *An Exhortation to Martyrdom*, SPCK 1979, p. 104.
17. Ibid., pp. 114ff.
18. Ibid., pp. 137–47.
19. Hans Urs von Balthasar, *Prayer*, SPCK 1973, passim.
20. Cf. Crouzel, op. cit., pp. 131–2.
21. Rowan Williams, *The Wound of Knowledge*, Darton, Longman and Todd 1979, p. 39.
22. Owen Chadwick, *John Cassian*, Cambridge University Press 1968, p. 85.
23. Charles Bigg, *The Christian Platonists of Alexandria*, Oxford University Press 1886, pp. 210, 212.

24. Cf. Philippians 3.4.
25. A. J. Malherbe and E. Ferguson (eds.) *Gregory of Nyssa*, Pantist Press 1978, p. 116.
26. Rowan Williams, 'Deification' in Gordon Wakefield (ed.), *A Dictionary of Christian Spirituality*, SCM Press 1983.
27. H. B. Workman, *Evolution of the Monastic Ideal*. References from K. E. Kirk, *The Vision of God*, Longmans 1932.
28. Owen Chadwick, op. cit., p. 68.
29. Ibid., p. 162.
30. Louth, op. cit., 1981, pp. 106ff.
31. Owen Chadwick, op. cit., pp. 104–9.
32. Ibid., p. 61.
33. Lilley, op. cit., p. 45.
34. Galatians 4.6.
35. J. Burnaby in A. R. Vidler (ed.), *Soundings*, Cambridge University Press 1962, pp. 235f.
36. D. Bonhoeffer, *The Psalms, Prayer Book of the Bible*, SLG Press, Fairacres, Oxford 1982, p. 8.
37. Bonhoeffer, ibid., passim.
38. Enzo Bianchi, *Concilium*, June 1990.
39. A. Schmemann, *Introduction to Liturgical Theology*, The Faith Press 1966, p. 109.
40. Romans 13.13–14.
41. Augustine, *Confessions*, trans. Henry Chadwick, 1991, VIII. vii–xii.
42. Ibid., X.xxix.
43. Ibid., IV.xiii.
44. Ibid., V.ii.
45. John 1.14, *Confessions*, X.xliii.
46. II Corinthians 5.15.
47. Andrew Louth, op. cit., pp. 136f.
48. Rowan Williams, op. cit., p. 73.
49. John Burnaby, *Amor Dei*, Hodder & Stoughton 1938, p. 71.
50. Quoted from Epistolare by Burnaby, ibid.
51. Rowan Williams, op. cit., p. 81.
52. John Burnaby, op. cit., pp. 63–66.
53. *Confessions*, X.xxxiii.
54. Quoted in Rowan Williams, op. cit., p. 88.
55. *Confessions*, X.vi.
56. John Burnaby, op. cit., p. 102.
57. Gerald Bonner, 'Augustine of Hippo' in Gordon Wakefield (ed.), *A Dictionary of Christian Spirituality*, SCM Press 1983.

58. Friedrich Heiler, *Prayer*, Oxford University Press 1932, p. 126.
59. J. W. C. Wand (ed.), *The City of God*, Oxford University Press 1963, p. 416.

3. The Medieval West

1. David N. Power, OM, 'Affirmed from Under: Celtic Liturgy and Spirituality', *Studia Liturgica*, Vol. 27, 1997 pp. 1ff.
2. Evelyn Underhill, *Mysticism*, Methuen 1930, p. 148.
3. Denys Turner, *The Darkness of God*, Cambridge University Press 1994, pp. 132–3.
4. J. R. H. Moorman, *A History of the Franciscan Order from its origins to the year 1517*, Oxford University Press 1968, p. 265.
5. Eamon Duffy, *The Stripping of the Altars*, Yale University Press 1992, p. 235.
6. Ibid.
7. Quoted by Leonard J. Bowman, 'Bonaventure and the Poetry of Gerard Manley Hopkins' S. Bonaventure 1274–1918 III, p. 557.
8. Duffy, op. cit., p. 121.
9. Ibid., p. 120.
10. K. W. Stevenson, *Eucharist and Offering*, Pueblo Publishing Company, New York, 1986, p. 90.
11. William Johnston, *Mystical Theology: The Science of Love*, HarperCollins 1995.
12. Demant, *A Two-Way Religion*, p. 24.
13. Turner, op. cit., pp. 142ff.
14. Cuthbert Butler, *Western Mysticism*, Constable, second edition 1926, p. lviii.
15. Quoted in Turner, op. cit., pp. 185, 273.
16. Ibid., p. 20.
17. Demant, op. cit., pp. 41f.
18. John Burnaby, *Amor Dei*, Hodder and Stoughton 1938, p. 3.
19. Cf. Bernard McGinn, *The Presence of God*, Vol. 2, pp. 32, 42, 48ff.
20. Turner, op. cit., p. 237.
21. Gallus, *Glossa* on Denys' *Mystical Theology* quoted in Turner, op. cit., p. 191.
22. W. R. Inge, *Christian Mysticism*, 1899, p. 140, quoted in Butler, op. cit., p. 96.
23. David Knowles, *The English Mystical Tradition*, Burns and Oates 1957, p. 124.
24. Butler, op. cit., pp. 105f.

25. Ibid., p. 126.
26. Turner, op. cit., p. 138.
27. Edmund Colledge and James Walsh (eds), Julian of Norwich, *Showings*, ed. Colledge and Walsh, Classics of Western Spirituality, Paulist Press 1978, pp. 293–6.
28. Butler, op. cit., p. 197.

4. The Eastern Church

1. Vladimir Lossky, *The Mystical Theology of the Eastern Church*, James Clarke 1957, pp. 8f.
2. A. G. Hebert, SSM (ed.), *The Parish Communion*, SPCK 1937, pp. 147f.
3. A. Schmemann, *Introduction to Liturgical Theology*, The Faith Press 1966, p. 13. Cf. Lossky op. cit., pp. 247ff.
4. Quoted in William Johnston, *Mystical Theology*, HarperCollins 1995, p. 77.
5. Lossky, op. cit., p. 213.
6. Ben Drewery, 'Deification' in Peter Brooks (ed.), *Christian Spirituality*, SCM Press 1975, pp. 33ff.; J. Burnaby, *Christian Words and Christian Meanings*, Hodder and Stoughton 1955; A. M. Allchin, *Participation in God*, Darton, Longman and Todd 1988, passim.
7. Lossky, op. cit., pp. 226f.
8. Hebert (ed.), op. cit., p. 303.

5. The Reformations

1. H. O. Evennett, *The Spirit of the Counter-Reformation*, Cambridge University Press 1968, p. 20.
2. Ibid., p. 51.
3. Roy Campbell, *Poems of St John of the Cross*, Harvill Press 1951.
4. Colin P. Thompson, *The Poet and the Mystic. A Study of the Cantico Espiritual of San Juan de la Cruz*, Oxford University Press 1977.
5. Colin P. Thompson, 'The Spanish Mystics' in Ralph Waller and Benedicta Ward (eds), *Introduction to Christian Spirituality*, SPCK 1999, p. 88.
6. Elizabeth Stopp, *St Francis de Sales*, Faber and Faber 1967.
7. Alister McGrath, *Roots that Refresh*, Hodder and Stoughton 1992.
8. E. Gordon Rupp, *Luther's Progress to the Diet of Worms*, SCM Press 1951, p. 28.
9. Calvin, *Institutes* 4.17.10.

10. John Bossy, *Christianity in the West*, Oxford University Press 1985, p. 115.
11. See my articles, 'Calvin, John' and 'Calvinist Spirituality' in *A Dictionary of Christian Spirituality*, SCM Press 1983.
12. See G. S. Wakefield, *Puritan Devotion*, Epworth Press 1957, pp. 85ff.
13. Richard Baxter, *Works*, XXIII, pp. 300–301.
14. John Stachniewski, *The Persecutory Imagination*, Clarendon Press 1991.
15. H. R. Trevor-Roper, *Catholics, Anglicans and Puritans*, Fontana 1987, p. ix.
16. G. S. Wakefield, *The Life of the Spirit in the World of Today*, Macmillan, New York and Epworth Press 1969, pp. 61–3.
17. Richard Ollard, *Clarendon and His Friends*, Hamish Hamilton 1987; Hugh Trevor-Roper, 'The Great Tew Circle in *Catholics, Anglicans and Puritans*, Fontana 1987.
18. Trevor-Roper, op. cit., p. 206.
19. E. Gordon Rupp, *Patterns of Reformation*, Epworth Press 1969, Part III.
20. Gordon Wakefield, *John Bunyan the Christian*, Harper Collins 1992 and Fount Harper Collins 1994.

6. From the Eighteenth Century to the Present

1. Much of this chapter was a contribution by Gordon S. Wakefield, and has been reproduced from Alister McGrath, *Encyclopedia of Modern Christian Thought*, Blackwell 1992, by kind permission of editor and publisher.
2. E. Gordon Rupp, *Religion in England 1688–1791*, Oxford University Press 1976, p. 207.
3. John Burnaby, *Amor Dei*, Hodder and Stoughton 1938, pp. 294ff.
4. R. W. Church, *Pascal and Other Sermons*, Macmillan and Co. 1896, p. 42.
5. G. F. Nuttall, *Richard Baxter and Philip Doddridge*, Oxford University Press 1951, passim.
6. D. Bruce Hindmarsh, *John Newton and the English Evangelical Tradition*, Clarendon Press 1996.
7. See Gordon S. Wakefield, *Methodist Spirituality*, Epworth Press 1999.
8. Ronald Knox, *Enthusiasm*, Clarendon Press 1950, p. 485.
9. J. H. Newman, *Essays Critical and Historical*, Vol. 1 quoted in Rupp, op. cit., p. 471.

10. See A. N. Wilson's important study, *God's Funeral*, Abacus 1999.

11. Ole Halesby, *Prayer*, Hodder & Stoughton p. 12.

12. Benedicta Ward, *Miracles and the Medieval Mind*, Wildwood House, 1986, p. 222.

13. Owen Chadwick, *The Spirit of the Oxford Movement*, Oxford University Press 1980, pp. 317ff.

14. John Burnaby, 'Christian Prayer' in A. R. Vidler (ed.), *Soundings*, Cambridge University Press 1962, pp. 221ff.

15. See Gordon S. Wakefield, *The Life of the Spirit in the World Today*, Epworth Press 1969, pp. 149f., for a fuller treatment of Balthasar and Rahner.

16. Gordon S. Wakefield, *Methodist Spirituality*, Epworth Press 1999.

17. Bonhoeffer, *Letters and Papers from Prison*, SCM Press 1953, pp. 154, 164.

18. Iris Murdoch, *The Sovereignty of Good*, Routledge and Kegan Paul, 1969, p. 55.

19. Michael Ramsey, *Sacred and Secular*, Longmans 1965, p. 45.

20. R. Gregor Smith, *Secular Christianity*, Collins 1966, see Wakefield 1969, pp. 125ff.

21. Bonhoeffer, op. cit., p. 103.

22. Peter Baelz, *Prayer and Providence*, SCM Press 1968, p. 88.

23. Ibid., pp. 100–101.

24. Ibid., p. 118.

25. John Burnaby, *Amor Dei*, Hodder and Stoughton 1938, p. 310; cf. Wakefield, *The Life of the Spirit*, pp. 146–9.

26. M. F. Wiles, *Reason to Believe*, SCM Press 1999.

27. Wiles, *Faith and the Mystery of God*, SCM Press 1982, pp. 126ff.

28. Wiles, *Reason to Believe*, p. 95ff.

29. Wiles, *Faith and the Mystery of God*, pp. 65ff.

Conclusion

1. Dominic Crossan, *The Historical Jesus*, T&T Clark 1991; Geza Vermes, *The Changing Faces of Jesus*, Penguin 2000.

2. R. C. Zaehner, 'Foolishness to the Greeks' (Oxford University Press 1955).

3. Gordon S. Wakefield, *The Life of the Spirit in the World of Today*, Macmillan, New York and Epworth Press 1969, pp. 65–9.

4. E.g., Maurice Wiles, *Reason to Believe*, SCM Press 1999,p. 95.

5. Dorothy Emmet, *Outward Forms, Inner Springs*, Macmillan 1998, p. 65.

6. Emmet, *The Effectiveness of Causes*, Macmillan 1984, pp. 111ff.
7. Iris Murdoch, *The Sovereignty of Good*, Routledge and Kegan Paul 1960, p. 55.
8. L. Gregory Jones and James J. Buckley (eds.), *Spirituality and Social Embodiment*, Blackwell 1997.
9. There has been further debate about this in *The Times Literary Supplement* in the early months of 2000. Van Dusen's book is *Dag Hammarskjöld: A Biographical Interpretation of Markings*, Faber and Faber 1967.
10. From *Old Creeds in a New World*, a radio statement by Hammarskjöld at the outset of his secretaryship, reprinted in Van Dusen, op. cit., pp. 46ff.

Bibliography

Spirituality in General

Louis Dupre and Don E. Saliers (eds), *Christian Spirituality: Post-Reformation and Modern*, Crossroad New York and SCM Press London 1989 sets Methodism in context and has an important section on 'Twentieth-century trajectories'.

Cheslyn Jones, Geoffrey Wainright and Edward Yarnold (eds), *The Study of Spirituality*, SPCK 1986

Ronald A. Knox, *Enthusiasm*, Oxford University Press 1950

Gordon Rupp, *Religion in England 1688–1791*, Oxford University Press 1986

Gordon S. Wakefield (ed.), *A Dictionary of Christian Spirituality*, SCM Press 1983

Methodism in general

E. S. Bucke (ed.), *A History of American Methodism*, 3 volumes, Abingdon Press 1964

Rupert E. Davies, *Methodism*, second revised edition, Epworth Press 1985

Rupert E. Davies, A. Raymond George and E. Gordon Rupp (eds), *A History of the Methodist Church in Great Britain*, 4 volumes, Epworth Press 1976–88

Thomas A. Langford, *Methodist Theology*, Epworth Press 1998

Henry D. Rack, *The Future of John Wesley's Methodism*, Lutterworth Press 1965

Gordon Rupp, *Principalities and Powers*, Epworth Press 1952

Barrie Tabraham, *The Making of Methodism*, Epworth Press 1995

W. J. Thompson, H. B. Workman and G. Eayrs (eds), *A New History of Methodism*, 2 volumes, Hodder and Stoughton 1909

J. Munsey Turner, *Conflict and Reconciliation*, Epworth Press 1985

J. Junsey Turner, *Modern Methodism in England 1932–1998*, Epworth Press 1998

John and Charles Wesley

Frank Baker, *Charles Wesley as revealed by his letters*, Epworth Press 1948

F. C. Gill, *Charles Wesley: The First Methodist*, Lutterworth Press 1964

Vivien H. H. Green, *The Young Mr Wesley*, Arnold 1961

Vivien H. H. Green, *John Wesley*, Nelson 1964

Richard P. Heizenrater, *The Elusive Mr Wesley*, 2 volumes, Abingdon Press 1984

Albert C. Outler, *John Wesley Selected Works*, Oxford University Press 1964. An anthology with a fine introduction.

Henry D. Rack, *Reasonable Enthusiast: Wesley and the Rise of Methodism*, Epworth Press 1989 and 1992. The definitive life.

Martin Schmidt, *John Wesley: A Theological Biography*, 2 volumes, Epworth Press 1962–73

John A. Vickers, *Charles Wesley*, Foundery Press 1990

Gordon S. Wakefield, *John Wesley*, Foundery Press 1989

F. L. Wiseman, *Charles Wesley Evangelist and Poet*, Epworth Press 1933

Methodist spirituality and worship

A. M. Allchin (ed.), *We Belong to One Another*, Epworth Press 1965

John C. Bowmer, *The Sacrament of the Lord's Supper in Early Methodism*, Dacre Press 1951

John C. Bowmer, *The Lord's Supper in Methodism 1791–1960*, Epworth Press 1961

Ted A. Campbell, *John Wesley and Christian Antiquity*, Kingswood Books 1991

W. E. Dutton, *The Eucharistic Manuals of John and Charles Wesley*, London 1871

W. E. Dutton, *John Wesley in Company with High Churchmen*, London 1869

R. Newton Flew, *The Idea of Perfection in Christian Theology*, Oxford University Press 1934

F. C. Gill, *John Wesley's Prayers*, Epworth Press 1951

T. S. Gregory, *According to Your Faith*, Epworth Press 1966

H. A. Hodges and A. M. Allchin, *A Rapture of Praise*, Hodder and Stoughton 1966

Harald Lindstrom, *Wesley and Sanctification*, Epworth Press 1950

George Osborn, *Poetical Works of John and Charles Wesley*, 13 volumes, Wesleyan Methodist Publishing House 1868–1872

Gordon S. Wakefield, *An Outline of Christian Worship*, T&T Clark 1998

Karen Westerfield Tucker (ed.), *The Sunday Service of the Methodists*, Kingswood 1996

Spiritual texts and influential studies

Richard Baxter, *The Saints' Everlasting Rest*, Caryl 1650, edited and abridged J. T. Wilkinson, Epworth Press 1962

Cuthbert Butler, *Western Mysticism*, Constable 1951

J. A. Chapman, *The Supernatural Life*, Epworth Press 1934

Giles Constable, *Three Studies in Medieval Religious and Social Thought*, Cambridge University Press 1995

J. A. Findlay, *Jesus and His Parables*, Epworth Press 1950

David F. Ford and Dennis L. Stamps, *Essentials of Christian Community*, T&T Clark 1996

A. Raymond George, *Communion with God in the New Testament*, Epworth Press 1953

William Law, *A Serious Call to a Devout and Holy Life*, 1728, many editions since including J. M. Dent 1906

Henry Lunn, *The Love of Jesus*, Hodder and Stoughton 1908

Henry Lunn, *Retreats for the Soul*, Hodder and Stoughton 1913

Henry Lunn, *The Secret of the Saints*, W. Heffer, Cambridge, 1933

W. R. Maltby, *Christ and His Cross*, Epworth Press 1935

Donald Nicholl, *Holiness*, Darton, Longman and Todd 1981, 1987, 1996

G. F. Nuttall, *The Puritan Spirit*, Epworth Press 1966

G. F. Nuttall, *The Holy Spirit in Puritan Faith and Experience*, Blackwell 1947 and Chicago 1992

W. E. Sangster, *The Path to Perfection*, Hodder and Stoughton 1943

W. E. Sangster, *The Pure in Heart*, Epworth Press 1954

Gordon S. Wakefield, *The Life of The Spirit in the World of Today*, Macmillan, New York and Epworth Press, London 1969

J. Neville Ward, *The Use of Praying*, Epworth Press 1967 and 1998

Leslie D. Weatherhead, *A Private House of Prayer*, Hodder and Stoughton 1958

Leslie D. Weatherhead, *The Christian Agnostic*, Hodder and Stoughton 1966

A. E. Whitham, *The Discipline and Culture of the Spiritual Life: A Memorial Volume compiled from his Writings*, Hodder and Stoughton 1938

Hymns

Henry Bett, *The Hymns of Methodism in their Literary Relations*, third edition, Epworth Press 1945

R. Newton Flew, *The Hymns of Charles Wesley: A Study of their Structure*, Epworth Press 1953

A. S. Gregory, *Praises with Understanding*, Epworth Press 1938ff.

Franz Hildebrandt and O. A. Beckerlegge with the assistance of James Dale, *A Collection of Hymns for the Use of the People called Methodists*, *The Works of John Wesley*, Volume 7, Clarendon Press, Oxford 1983

Bernard L. Manning, *The Hymns of Wesley and Watts*, Epworth Press 1942

J. E. Rattenbury, *The Evangelical Doctrines of Charles Wesley's Hymns*, Epworth press 1941

J. R. Rattenbury, *The Eucharistic Hymns of John and Charles Wesley*, Epworth Press 1948

J. R. Watson, *The English Hymn*, Clarendon Press, Oxford 1997

Worthies

A Memoir of Joseph Entwistle by his Son, Mason 1848ff.

W. Bardsley Brash, *Love and Life, The Story of J. Denholm Brash by his Son*, Kelly 1913

Samuel Coley, *Life of Thomas Collins*, Jobson 1869

Norman G. Dunning, *Samuel Chadwick*, Epworth Press 1933

Brian Frost, *Goodwill on Fire: the Life of Donald Soper*, Hodder and Stoughton 1996

Joseph Nettleton, *John Hunt*, London undated c.1900

Paul Sangster, *Dr Sangster*, Epworth Press 1962

Luke Tyerman, *Praying William*, Mason 1857

J. A. Vickers (ed.), *Wisdom and Wit, An Anthology from the Writings of Gordon Rupp*, Methodist Publishing House undated

Gordon S. Wakefield, *Robert Newton Flew*, Epworth Press 1971

Gordon S. Wakefield, *T. S. Gregory*, Teamprint, Loughborough 1999

Kingsley Weatherhead, *Leslie Weatherhead*, Hodder and Stoughton 1975

J. T. Wilkinson, *William Clowes*, Epworth Press 1951

J. T. Wilkinson, *Hugh Bourne* Epworth Press 1952

Articles

J. H. B. Andrews, 'The Rise of the Bible Christians', *The Preacher's Quarterly*, March 1965, p. 58.

T. H. Barratt, *London Quarterly Review*, July 1923

O. A. Beckerlegge, *London Quarterly and Holborn Review*, October 1964

Henry Bett, 'The Origins of the Class Meeting', *Wesley Historical Society Proceedings*, 1931, pp. 41ff.

J. A. Findlay, 'Can we be "Friends of Sinners" and yet separate from them?', *The Preacher's Quarterly*, December 1954

A. Raymond George, 'Private Devotion in the Methodist Tradition', *Studia Liturgica*, Vol. II no. 3, September 1963, p. 233.

T. S. Gregory, 'They Shall See God', *Manuals* 1926

T. S. Gregory, 'The Compassion of Jesus', *Manuals* 1929

T. R. and W. R. Maltby, 'Studies in St Mark 1–4', *Manuals of Fellowship*, Epworth Press 1920ff.

John A. Newton, 'Methodism and the Puritans', Dr Williams' Library lecture 1964

Gordon Rupp, 'Methodism and the Protestant Tradition', Epworth Press 1951

Gordon Rupp, 'A Devotion of Rapture in English Puritanism' in R. Buick Knox (ed.), *Reformation, Conformity and Dissent*, Epworth Press 1997, pp. 115ff.

Gordon Wakefield, 'Methodist Union: Youthful Memories, Adult Assessment and Future Hopes', *Epworth Review*, May 1982, p. 30

Select bibliography

William Johnston, *'Arise my Love' Mysticism for a New Era*, Orbis Books 2000

Cheslyn Jones, Geoffrey Wainwright and Edward Yarnold (eds), *The Study of Spirituality*, SPCK 1986

Alister McGrath, *Roots that Refresh*, Hodder and Stoughton 1992

C. A. Patrides (ed.), *The Cambridge Platonists*, Cambridge University Press 1980

Gordon S. Wakefield (ed.), *A Dictionary of Christian Spirituality*, SCM Press 1983

J. Neville Ward, *The Use of Praying*, Epworth Press 1967, 1999
Rowan Williams, *The Wound of Knowledge*, Darton, Longman and Todd
1979

Gordon Wakefield served for over fifty years as a Methodist minister. He was successively Connexional Editor, responsible for the Epworth Press; Chairman of the Manchester and Stockport District; and Principal of the ecumenical Queen's College, Birmingham. He was the first Methodist to be awarded the Lambeth DD His previous works include: *Puritan Devotion*; *Methodist Devotion*; *An Outline of Christian Worship*; *Kindly Light: Meditations on Newman's Poem*; *The Liturgy of St John*; and *Bunyan the Christian*. He died on September 11th, 2000.

Index